A Clearing
in the Wilderness

OTHER BOOKS BY HUGH FOSBURGH

The Hunter
View from the Air
The Sound of White Water
The Drowning-Stone
One Man's Pleasure
The Good Chance

A Clearing
in the Wilderness

BY HUGH FOSBURGH

GARDEN CITY, NEW YORK
DOUBLEDAY & COMPANY, INC.
1969

Introduction

Baker's Clearing and the Baker Tract on which it is located are in the remote central Adirondacks. The tract is surrounded by the state-owned Forest Preserve, square mile after square mile of wilderness—which by constitutional decree "shall be forever kept as wild forest lands." The nearest permanent neighbors of the clearing are ten mountainous, tenuous dirt-road miles away and, except for a fire tower on Blue Mountain, twenty miles distant, there is no man-made thing to be seen, or sensed. So Baker's Clearing is a little world unto itself, detached from reality perhaps, serene, almost a dream place.

The clearing came into being in 1854, when Squire Thomas Baker, his wife, two daughters, and a hired man arrived with some assorted livestock, and undertook the classic life of pioneers. While they went about the torturous process of converting seventy acres of virgin wilderness into a clearing that would sustain horses, cows, and sheep, and a vegetable garden, and a

*The clearing, as Eliphalet Terry painted it in
1869. There is no trace of the buildings de-
picted here and the present-day house and
barns are on higher ground to the left.*

plot of flowers of course, Baker and the hired man peeled hemlock bark for the tanneries to the south, shot deer and caught
trout not only to eat but also for the market, trapped mink and
otter, and waged a holding war against the wolves.

Soon after their arrival, Mrs. Baker started a boardinghouse
to which devoted customers—mostly bachelor artists and literary
people from New York, Boston, and Albany—came year after
year. (It was in these years that many city-oriented people
developed a fascination for the frontier and the wilderness so
that a new romantic art and literature—the American Scene—
came into being.)

Juliet, one of Baker's daughters, started a diary in 1862 and
continued it, with daily entries, for twenty-five years—in its
cryptic, understated way it records with marvelous clarity the
important happenings on the clearing. She was also the family
bookkeeper and correspondent, and she tucked away all the

*One hundred and fifteen years later—the stumps
are gone but nothing else has basically changed.*

accounts and letters that she received, so that there is today
a valid impression of their way of life.

Starting in 1867 and continuing through the early 1900s, two
painters, Eliphalet Terry and his more illustrious friend, Winslow
Homer, were recording the scene with love and understanding.
It is evident from their pictures that it hasn't changed much,
basically, to this day; it is still the same remote clearing in the
same wilderness.

After Squire Baker died and when his wife and daughters had
moved nine miles closer to civilization, some of their devoted
boarders bought the tract and formed an association which continues through their descendants to this day. My grandfather
was one of them and that is how I happen to be there.

When I say that the clearing hasn't basically changed, I do
not mean that we live under the primitive isolated circumstances
of the Bakers—we have a sometime telephone; we cut logs with

Circa 1875—three boarders at Baker's Clearing, photographed by Terry. They are well accoutered and staunchly determined to face any eventuality.

a chain saw instead of chopping the trees down with an ax; we use delicate trout flies and not the gaudy improbable creations that were no doubt just as efficacious; we get about in jeeps and Land Rovers instead of buckboards; we truck our logs to market instead of driving them down the river; we hunt game for the pleasure of it, not from necessity; and we refrigerate our food instead of cutting ice on Mink Pond. So life is easier and we are more comfortable and secure, but if Mr. Terry or Mr. Homer were to return today, I think they would feel at ease and be content with what they found.

My cottage is in the most secluded corner of the clearing and each room has great windows that face in various directions. I spend a wicked lot of time looking out those windows and the choice of which one depends mostly on the season and the time of day.

The living room, for instance, faces north and west, outside are the lower clearing and the evergreen swamp, and beyond is the rolling wilderness that sweeps in a great arc from Blue Mountain to Beaver Mountain. This prospect is best in warm weather and it is particularly fine of an early morning in June, with the sun coming up and the mist rising from the ponds and river, when there's a quiet ecstasy of bird song and swallows are skimming over the pasture.

The library window faces south, overlooking my poverty-grass rock-studded "lawn" ("lawn" means that I've finally tamed it sufficiently so that I don't have to hand-scythe it, except in certain places). The big prolific wild apple tree is in the center of it, and beyond is an alder swale, and beyond that, sloping up to the beech woods, is another corner of the pasture. Keeping vigilance at this window is pleasing in all kinds of inclement or cold weather, especially in winter, because the outlook is small and protected, never overpowering with far bleak expanses of snow. It's a nice place to sit with a book or drink tea with a friend.

That apple tree is my pride and pleasure, and the joy also of many other things—bluebirds and hummingbirds nest in it, and sapsuckers are forever probing the bark, and in blossom time a hoard of honey bees and bumblebees minister to it with absorbed devotion, but it is the deer and the coons who are periodically obsessed by it. The deer start sniffing around in mid-July, when there is some small hope that one or two green measly apples will have dropped off; by the end of August there is an erratic procession coming to it, and by October they are haunting it. (One fall a selfish old doe literally lived and slept beneath it trying to monopolize the bounty—she roused herself whenever an apple plopped down, but she was overwhelmed by sheer numbers).

Having the deer about the tree is pure delight, but the coons,

From the library window—the deer have had a temporary glut of apples and are heading for the alder swale.

equally gluttonous, are something yet again—they vandalize the tree by breaking down the branches with their weight. Three autumns ago, there was a veritable plague of coons (the next spring a disease killed most of them), and late one afternoon, sitting at the window, I watched three litters, totaling fourteen coons, scramble into the tree and begin to devastate it. That was too much for me—I went there, climbed up, and shook them all out, taking malicious satisfaction as each one came whomping down.

A small colony of snowshoe rabbits live under the house and go in and out through a hole that is directly beneath the library window. One sparkling moonlit night in January, I was sitting there in darkness, mesmerized by the stillness and by the moon that was like a glaring wafer, when four of them, white as the snow itself, emerged from the hole and went dashing onto the lawn. They engaged in frantic rabbit games, chasing each other madly, cutting fancy impromptu capers, leaping and twisting high in the air like demented ghostly ballet dancers. It still isn't wholly real to me, but it happened.

The alder swale and the pasture beyond are a natural crossing place for a variety of animals; they come up through the valley from the river, cross the height of land at its lowest point, drop down through the beech woods to the pasture and swale, and from thence down into the low pond country. Deer use it the year round, and especially during the fall rut; one November afternoon I saw a big doe bust out of the beeches and career across the pasture into the alders, then seconds later a buck followed in belching pursuit, then a second buck raced out, and finally a third—a monstrous bellowing animal—came pounding along. By the time everything was quiet again, I was shaking with excitement.

Otters and foxes and coyotes use the crossing too. Coyotes, when they come into the pasture, often pause and mill about while they yap and yowl, making a din like the hounds of hell.

From the office window—Beaver Mountain.

And sometimes a single animal will come there and sit, and set up an eerie wailing that is all lonely grief and chilling mystery.

The bay window upstairs in my office-bedroom facing east, is my favorite, and I fritter away more time there, doing haphazard sentry duty, than at any other. Directly below the window are the salt licks and the bird feeder and the meat caches, and just beyond is the evergreen forest that slopes down to the swamp. In the near distance is the pond country and beyond, like a giant Buddha, is Beaver Mountain.

Sitting at the work table by the window, I feel like a lord—everything around and about is mine, even Beaver Mountain is mine—it is all a stage set for my personal convenience and pleasure, there is constant entertainment, and I can partake of it whenever I choose.

The salt licks and the bird feeder are in operation the year round. Originally the licks—various kinds of salt blocks placed on rotting stumps—were intended for the deer, but I soon discovered that certain species of birds—finches, grosbeaks, siskins, and crossbills—were also greatly addicted to them, especially in winter. It's a gay, lively occasion when an assortment of birds, twittering and squeaking and squawking, jockey for a place on one of the licks.

The meat caches are to lure the predators—foxes, coyotes, bobcats, fisher, mink, weasels, and bears, also owls and hawks —but I operate them only in winter because at other times coons would monopolize them, and the fewer the coons there are around the house, the better I like it. I use whatever meat is available, mostly the carcasses of starved deer and trapped beaver. I hang some in trees, for the climbers, and put the others on snow mounds.

This assortment of devices makes for interesting times out there, and occasionally something spectacular occurs. There was the time I watched a red fox make a patient Machiavellian stalk on a red squirrel eating on the bird feeder—the fox pounced and missed, then slowly trotted off, feigning total unconcern, and minutes later the squirrel was back on the feeder, also unconcerned.

And one day in early April, I glanced out to see a great black bear—the very grubbiest dirtiest rankest bear you would ever

A salt stump and red crossbills.

Bluejay.

see outside of a zoo—directly under the window. I hallooed to him, and he stopped to look up at me over his shoulder. Maybe he was dopey from his winter's sleep, or maybe he just didn't give two beans for me or anything else—anyway he turned and went slouching down to the swamp.

And there was the time when I thought, for a confusing moment, that I was out of my mind—a part of a beaver carcass that I had out there on a snow mound seemed to be moving towards me. It *was,* and then I saw what was propelling it; a white weasel, going backward, had hold of it, and was tugging it along with furious energy toward a small opening under the house. It succeeded in this but couldn't get its prize through the opening, which made it quiver and sputter with frustration. Subsequently, and for about six weeks, I had some delightful times with this diabolical, evil-tempered thing—I attached a wire to the beaver carcass, and whenever I pulled the wire from my upstairs window, the weasel would screetch out from under the house, seize the carcass, and worry it back to the opening.

The prospect from this window, or any of the windows, is not always pleasing and lovely—it is sometimes grim as only nature can be. There was that brutal winter of '58–'59 when there was no need to put out meat caches—the fierce cold and heavy snow came in late November and continued unabated through February. The weaker deer started dying by New Year's and two weeks later there were three dead ones within sight of the office window. Then one morning an old old doe wallowed out from the balsams and lay down by the salt licks. For a long time she lay there with her head swaying gently back and forth, like an old lady dropping off to sleep in her armchair, then her head settled back on her shoulder and she never moved again. Her carcass—everything except the stomach, the hair, and a few bones—was gone in a month.

I am a poor sleeper and sometimes, in some places, the nights seem long. But never at Baker's Clearing—when I am safe in bed, the night sounds are all pleasurable and familiar and reassuring, so I don't mind at all being woken by any of them—the squashy crunch of a deer eating apples twenty feet away; the booming of the bullfrogs and the calling of the loons on

Mink Pond; a barred owl pontificating about nothing at all; on a still winter night, the boom of ice cracking on the ponds, like far-off cannon fire; the flute music of the wind around the eaves; the coyotes' wailing. (Perhaps to be woken by the coyotes is best of all.) And then there are those nights that can come only in the wilderness—the moonless windless nights, when the world is in suspense and there is no sound at all, nothing—just portentous overwhelming dark. That too can stir me from sleep.

Whenever I leave the clearing for an extended period, it is with foreboding and a feeling of guilt—something sinister will surely happen while I'm gone—so I make a quick, surreptitious departure. And when I come back, after months, it is always a small miracle—Baker's Clearing is just as I left it.

*A Clearing
in the Wilderness*

Mink Pond—rotting ice.

Spring

1.

At Baker's Clearing, we celebrate New Year's in the usual festive way, but the day itself doesn't mean much. To us, a far more important day comes in late April or early May when the ice goes out of Mink Pond; that is when the winter death grip is broken and the new year *really* begins.

Winter on the tract comes early and lasts a long long time—so long, finally, it seems interminable. December through February is an exhilarating time—there is a sharp challenge that makes you feel ten feet tall, but by mid-March the winter has gone stale and you've gone stale with it—you've had all the cold and snow and ice you need or want. By April winter is dragging on like a senile cantankerous bear that refuses to die—it's moody one day, vicious the next, proffering false hopes the one after that, then mean again; there's an arbitrary, seemingly calculated deviltry that taxes all patience.

So we look forward with childish anticipation to the ice going out of Mink—we speculate endlessly on the date, and make up a pool on it, and give out wise predictions, each one based on personal and authoritative experience which no one else has acquired, and which are consistently fallacious. I, personally, make an almost daily inspection trip, thinking I can hurry up the process by taking an interest and demonstrating my impatience, but it's like the pot that won't boil.

Nevertheless, these afternoon excursions on snowshoes to the pond are always interesting, not just in noting the wretched ice situation, but in seeing what the wild things have been doing about the shore. The places where the water has opened up—the inlet and the south-facing shore are the first spots to go—have an attraction for almost all birds and animals. Ducks, both the divers that are going north and the puddles that are apt to stay and nest, congregate there. So do the grackles and blackbirds. These latter anticipate spring by as much as two months and why they come back so soon or how they survive the snow and miserable environment I don't know, but there they are, seemingly unconcerned and cheerful.

The inlet is a fine place to see just about any kind of animal, or at least indications that it has been there. Once, from far off, I saw something on the ice, just at the water's edge, that looked like a black bushel basket turned upside down—it was a great beaver humped there, doing nothing whatever so far as I could tell, but it was a bright afternoon so I presume it was sunning itself. Another time, I watched four otters fishing in the mud for small frogs and polliwogs and crayfish; they would leap out on the ice to savor whatever they'd found, then slip back into the water again; then they played tag in and out of the water like kids in a swimming hole, except they didn't make any noise about it. And still another time, I came on the tracks of a big bear; he had gone straight to the open channel, flopped himself in, swum across and slogged ashore, leaving behind an important trail of ooze.

There are always deer about the inlet, not only because it is a wintering area for them but also because they have a fascination for rotten ice. Deer are absolute asses when it comes to bad ice—like teen-age boys, they keep testing it until they break

The loons are back.

through, and then they can be in trouble. Sometimes real trouble. A few years ago, a buck came out of the swamp and tried to cross the ice, and broke through—as any moron could have foreseen. His plight thereafter was plain to see and pitiful—he had crashed an erratic, jagged channel across the inlet, leaving much blood and clots of hair, then finally crawled out on the far bank and slumped in exhaustion. I found him there dead— of pneumonia probably.

The death of this animal was most gratifying to the carnivores; in no time various coyotes, bobcats, fisher, mink, foxes, and weasels found out about him and feasted, and one day there was a goshawk sitting on the carcass, so gorged it could barely heave itself into the air.

Except for the inlet and the south-facing shore, the ice goes out of Mink all at once, in a single day. There is something incredible about it—for weeks you've been watching it, pristine at first under a cover of dry snow, then turning gray as the snow becomes slush, and then for days it just sits there, sullen and treacherous and hateful and apparently everlasting—and then one day, presto, it's gone like a bad dream. And just as quickly, looking at the black clear pond with the pair of loons fishing in the deep water, you have a new outlook; you put out of mind the grim winter realities such as the predators feeding on the buck carcass, and dwell on the new delightful circumstances that have developed. There are trout in the pond out there that will be voracious after the lean time under the ice; and you can put away the snowshoes and the long johns and get out the canoe and the bluejeans; and any day now the tree swallows will be back, lively and blythe and confident; and that dull distant-thunder sound that has been intruding is a partridge drumming for a mate; and on the way home you can look hopefully for those tiny yellow violets that are the first flowers to peek up in the sunny places; and surely tonight, just before total dark, woodcock will be mating in the alder swamp by the house—the males making yanking, sour nasal sounds, then launching upward and out of sight, twittering, into the night sky, then plummeting down on their mates.

What I've been describing is that not unusual thing called "spring fever"—but on Baker's Clearing we get virulent attacks of it.

The date of ice-out on Mink is erratic—it can come as early as April 20 or as late as the tenth of May, and the progression of spring thereafter, in a meteorological way, is also unpredictable, but if a man had no calendar or way of keeping track of time, he could make a fairly accurate appraisal by noting the arrival of migrating birds—whatever the weather, the first-comers of each species keep an almost precise schedule, year after year.

From December until mid-February there will be only the resident winter birds—chickadees, bluejays, evening grosbeaks, and various kinds of woodpeckers, nuthatches, and owls (every few years these will be augmented by invasions of crossbills, redpolls, pine grosbeaks, and siskins from the northern boreal zone), and then, on or about the fifteenth of February, you're bound to see some gross cowbirds on the feeder. An occasional horned lark will appear almost simultaneously and sit morosely on the snow, as though it had second thoughts about its early return.

The shadbush blooms.

Goshawks are on their nesting sites, and screeching at intruders, by March 10 and the first blackbirds and grackles are in Mink inlet and the open brooks at the same time.

Within two days of March 20 you can count on the first song sparrow, robin, and bluebird, followed within three days by hermit thrushes.

About April 18 you wake up on a brisk sunny morning knowing instantly that spring is here to stay (it usually isn't), because there is a proliferation of new birds on the clearing; flickers are making ardent loud love forays, sapsuckers are pounding away on any resonant insulator or tin roof, tree swallows are inspecting the nesting boxes, whitethroats and myrtle warblers and kinglets are learning to sing, and fox sparrows are scratching with the determination of chickens underneath the bird feeder.

Loon eggs.

(For some of these birds, especially the swallows, a late snow-storm or cold wave can create a desperate situation.)

After this, there are so many birds on and about the clearing that it is impossible to keep track of the new arrivals, but about May 25, and continuing for several days, there comes the bird watcher's delight—the spring migration of the warblers—a twittering flitting gregarious gay pilgrimage of tiny intense birds, trending north along the stream sides and through the mountain passes. They are in no frantic hurry—rather it's as though they're picnicking along the way—but they have a vague purpose and a final destination. Soon the main body passes along and the others disperse to nest, and the climax of spring is over.

2.

If you're a logger, there comes a time in spring after the snow has mostly gone and before the trees leaf out, when you have to bring all woods operations to a halt. This is "mud season," and it is the time to overhaul your machinery and to go over your books to see how you came out on the winter's job.

Black-backed woodpecker at its nesting hole.

It is also an excellent time to cruise timber—to get about the woods and decide where and what you are going to cut next, to estimate the amount and quality of it, to spot out the proposed cutting areas and haul roads, and to assess generally what sort of an operation it is going to be. You can do this survey at any time of year except summer—when the foliage hinders the perspective—but autumn is a hectic time for a logger, and in winter you have to travel on snowshoes and can't tell exactly the hard ground from the wet places—an important thing to know when you're laying out roads. So early spring is the ideal time for it.

There have been lumbering operations on the Baker Tract for over a hundred years—from the time that Squire Baker moved there. He cut hemlock for tannery bark, leaving the logs to rot, and, like all lumbermen, he occasionally "lost" some of his product—which is to say that he cut it, and then for some reason failed to get it out of the woods—and I know where there are presently six great stacks of hemlock bark which, if you peel off the top layers, is still as sound as the day he piled it there.

Subsequently and for three decades, various loggers cut pine and spruce either on or adjacent to the tract—Frank, Thumb,

Circa 1885—Frank Pond after the loggers have gone.

Huntley, Nate, and Dunk ponds, and Blackwell's Stillwater, on the river, are all named after lumbermen who had operations in their particular vicinity. In the 1890s and up to 1909, Rob Bibby had three different camps on the tract and logged off the last of the virgin softwood.

This sounds like a terrible carnage and no doubt it was, but the true, almost incredible thing about it is that today there is little evidence that it happened, or even that hoards of men had worked their will. Forty years ago, for instance, there were the moldering remains of a three-story log shanty that Bibby's crew lived in for two years, but there isn't a trace of it today—the site is overgrown by a mature stand of balsam; for years there was the iron shoe of a great wagon wheel leaning against a maple tree at Dunk LaPrairie's camp, but the last time I looked I had a hard time finding it—the tree had fallen down and the shoe had disintegrated so that I could break it apart with my hands; near the spring at Frank May's shanty there was a great beech in which at least thirty men had carved their initials, but it too has fallen down and rotted away. And there was another of Bibby's camps on Apple Tree Brook—so named because he planted an apple tree there—the tree survived for years and produced small rock-hard fruit, then finally the fast-growing balsam shaded it to death and there's no trace of it today, and almost no trace that Bibby lived there and ravaged the forest. You can find the massive rotten pine stumps, some of them six feet in diameter, and in a few swampy ravines, you can use your imagination and knowledge of logging to surmise where Bibby probably had his tote road to the river, then if you are sufficiently interested, you can grub down through the leaves and mold and muck to discover, almost surely, the corduroy remains. This is all the tangible evidence there is—frail inconsequential reminders that men had been there, and prevailed briefly, and passed along.

There is a fine romantic and erroneous conception of the primeval Adirondack wilderness—it was a sublime place, teeming with food and game, an Eden. It was not—the massive and magnificent climax timber made for a virtual woodland desert —a great overstory of trees that shaded to death the upstart

Frank Pond today.

growth beneath. It is not happenstance that most Indians shunned the Adirondacks and that the few who lived there permanently were called "Bark Eaters," and were scorned by other Indians. When Squire Baker moved to the tract, he was hard-pressed to kill deer, which was a meat staple in his household; he jacked them on the ponds at night, he hounded them, he dug pitfalls and set snares, and ran them down in deep snow, and every successful effort was worthy of mention in his daughter's terse diary.

That the Adirondacks, down through the centuries, weren't perpetually a forest wasteland was primarily due to natural disasters—fire and storm. In 1867, for instance, a fire raged all summer on the tract—it started near Blackwell's Stillwater, burned east across Splitrock Pond, and up the western slope of Beaver Mountain, where it finally burned out—and all the while this was going on, it caused no inconvenience to the Bakers, except for a pall of smoke, and no concern. Forty years later, exactly, another fire swept most of the same area, but today that land is producing as vigorous timber as there is on the tract, and teems with game.

On November 20, 1950, there came the so-called "blowdown storm"—a wild, eerie day and night during which thousands of acres of Adirondack timber land were flattened and decimated. It turned out eventually, and in most instances, to be a dis-

Circa 1900—a place near the clearing, after logging.

The exact same place today—the overage balsam pulp has been cut to make growing room for the white pine, but it is already shading to death all the young growth. Ecologically it is once again a woodland desert.

guised blessing—through the awful jumble of overthrown trees, a burgeoning young growth arose, creating circumstances where all kinds of Adirondack wildlife can prosper, not just woodpeckers and owls and wood mice and red squirrels and porcupines, and other such deep-woods species.

Perhaps the lesson to be learned is that Adirondack forests have an incredible capacity to rejuvenate themselves, and it doesn't much matter whether this rejuvenation is created by loggers or by the violence of nature—except that loggers are

This is the situation less than fifty yards from where the two previous pictures were taken. The "blow-down" storm of 1950 struck hard here, letting in the light, so that today it's a haven for wildlife and a burgeoning forest.

required by law to alleviate the after-hazard of fire, whereas a blowdown storm can make tinderbox conditions that last for decades.

There is a popular illusion about Adirondack loggers, in fact all loggers everywhere, that rankles me—they are reputed to be evil, greedy, ruthless, destroying brigands. A New York *Times* editorial once referred to them, in toto, as "malefactors of destruction." I resent it—I have been a logger for twenty years, and I have known dozens of them, and I think damn few of us fit the description—most of us have been drawn to it because we had a natural affinity for the out-of-doors and especially the woods, and not because we had easy get-rich-quick prospects in view.

What many people tend to forget, or dismiss, is one basic fact—if you're going to live in, and from, the wilderness, it necessarily entails destroying some part of it. To make a living and survive, you can't just sit there and have lovely thoughts about it—you've got to kill some things, be they trees or buffalo or passenger pigeons, or beaver. But to many people it doesn't matter that the beaver trappers—the "mountain men"—were hugely responsible for the exploration that made possible our westward expansion; it doesn't matter that the buffalo hunters perpetrated a massacre that made possible the beef ranches of today, or that the farmers and homesteaders of the '60s and '70s, who slaughtered the pigeons, performed a necessary service to the grain farmers of today; it doesn't matter that loggers produced the wood that made homes and newspapers and railroad ties—what matters and is remembered, and unforgiven, is that these people were destroyers and therefore innately despicable. Phooey, I say.

After the clean-cutting of all the climax softwood timber on the tract, Rob Bibby built a water-powered sawmill on Mink outlet, just below the pond, and for forty-five years it turned out the lumber for all construction on the tract. It was a minor operation in relation to the available timber—second growth softwood and mature hardwoods—so that when we started to market

Malefactors of destruction—John Baker and his sawmill crew. Lumbermen constitute the backbone of Adirondack economy and a distinctive way of life, but to some uninvolved people this couldn't matter less.

logs and pulpwood in 1938, there was available at least twenty million feet of mature or overmature timber.

In those first years, during the war, we sold wood as an act of desperation—to pay taxes and basic expenses. We barely succeeded because no one was in effective control and the operation was in charge of inept fly-by-night operators who had difficulty meeting their basic expenses, let alone paying stumpage charges to us. It was a wasteful, sordid operation, and when it was done, four hundred acres of fine timberland had been cut over with small benefit to anyone, but it taught us an invaluable lesson—how *not* to conduct a logging operation—and today, twenty-five years later, that acreage is bountiful forestland.

Since that sorry experience, we haven't made many mistakes, in fact we haven't done anything for which, as yet, we are truly sorry.

*Howard Martindale, log roller, left, and Milton
Hutchins, sawyer.*

Before we started logging in 1938, the timber situation on the
tract was similar to that on the Forest Preserve lands which
surround it; almost everywhere, except where natural disasters
had occurred, it was a climax forest. Soon afterward a notable
difference became apparent; the tract evolved into a thriving
vibrant place, ecologically, and the young timber flourished,
whereas on the Forest Preserve lands the situation remained
static and stagnant. (The Forest Preserve, by state law, "shall
remain forever wild and free.") This law was promulgated
more than seventy years ago with the very best intention—to
preserve it for posterity—but I have come to wonder whether
at certain times and in certain places it could be better pre-
served and more productive of all life, and just as wild, by
some judicious timbering.

At any rate, on the Baker Tract we try to run an economically practical and sustaining operation; the basic wilderness is still there, but it is even more exciting and vital than before.

There is no feasible way to do a logging job that doesn't leave the woods looking frightful; no matter how you go about it, there is the aftermath of treetops and slash and skid paths, but what many people do not know is that when you cut a stand of timber in the Adirondacks it reseeds immediately and matures quickly. A balsam or a poplar, for instance, can be overmature and beginning to rot at fifty years; a white pine can be prime and three-plus feet in butt diameter at sixty years; hardwoods take longer to mature—seventy years or more—but

it isn't long afterward that they will begin to stagnate, with the wolf trees shading out the less hardy ones. So a cut-over woodland doesn't maintain that battleground appearance for long—first come the ferns and the raspberry briars, and the treetops and debris rot to the ground, the young growth rises through the briars, and then a vast assortment of wildlife find things to their liking, and once again it is a thriving exciting place.

"Selective cutting" is a phrase much used by foresters and conservationists, but it has little applicability on the Baker Tract simply because the timber on the areas we cut is either prime or overmature or decadent so it would make no sense to cut one tree here and another there—far better to take everything and get out, and leave the forest to recoup, than to go back time and again and reopen old wounds.

Despite the complaints of many forest-loving people that loggers destroy everything and put nothing back (in certain timber situations in North America this is undoubtedly true) it is wholly unnecessary and would be arrant folly for us to attempt to replant cut-over areas. The seeds of natural rebirth on the tract are so strong that we have to wage a continual holding action to keep our basic seventy-acre clearing from reverting to wilderness, so any attempt we might make to influence what grew up on cut-over land would be presumptuous and ineffective—it would burgeon, and prevail in its own way, despite our mightiest efforts.

What we cut, and where, depends largely on what timber is accessible and merchantable, and is either stagnant or deteriorating. When we started logging in 1946—after that first wartime fiasco—there was a great stand of softwood timber that swept through the low-lying country from Thumb Pond inlet to Frank Pond and Beaver Outlet. Much of this was overage balsam, suitable for pulpwood, and since the price for it was adequate (I never knew of a pulp and paper company that paid more than a barely adequate price for the raw material) we concluded to start there. This area comprised a traditional deer-wintering area—one of the largest in the Adirondacks—and the fact that cutting it would greatly benefit the browse situation was a big factor in the decision. Anyway, we began at the clearing and cut west around Lower Beaver toward Frank Pond, making a permanent all-weather truck road as we went. We didn't cut the mature pine, hoping it would dominate the reseeding process, and we left behind pockets of softwood that would give weather protection to the deer. We were successful in both of these efforts—today the young pines are twenty feet high and growing at the rate of three feet a year, and the deer are, at least temporarily, living in fairly secure circumstances. In ten years the browse will be above their reach and they will once again be living in a ghetto situation—until we make another cut.

Cutting pulp is a meat-and-potatoes operation. If you are efficient about it, you can rest assured that it's going to bring in the basic wherewithal, but you also know that you're not going to get rich doing it. It's like clipping blue-ribbon bonds and being guaranteed your 4 per cent.

We cut pulp in the Lower Beaver area for four years—about eight hundred cords a year. We did this mostly in summer and fall, when the ground was relatively dry and firm, because in those days, the cutting and yarding of pulp was a one-man one-horse operation, and skidding tree-length poles on boggy ground or in deep snow is unnecessarily rough on both man and horse. (Today woods horses in the Adirondacks have been almost entirely replaced by tractors, more's the pity, which are effective almost any place and at any time of year except spring, so that it doesn't much matter where or when you operate.) We netted enough money at least to pay our taxes.

Coincident with this basic operation, we cut hardwood logs in the late fall and winter—mostly yellow birch and hard maple and beech. A hardwood job is not the safe dependable thing that a pulp job is. For one thing, you can't cruise a stand of hardwood and come up with an almost exact estimate of what the final tally will be, the way you can pulp. You can't assess the amount and quality of the timber until you cut the trees down and saw them into logs. Also, any lumberjack who knows how to use a chain saw and a horse can put up pulp for you— all he has to do is cut the tree down, trim it, yard it, cut it into four-foot lengths, and pile it—but there is nothing so cut and dried about turning out hardwood logs. A team of careful and knowledgeable men can do a successful job in a stand of inferior timber where a bunch of hackers would make a dismal failure of it. Furthermore, the market for pulp has been constant and the price almost unchanging (in the twenty-odd years we have been selling it the price hasn't changed 10 per cent, which in these days of inflation makes me wonder how the companies contrive to keep it that way), but none of these circumstances hold true with the marketing of logs. It is a highly speculative proposition. To be sure, the value for choice hard maple and yellow birch has risen steadily since the war—in 1941 we were getting four dollars per thousand board feet of standing birch, whereas in 1961 we were getting $110 per thousand for logs of similar quality—almost twenty-six times as much. But there are risks—having to do with a speculative market and with the fact that you're dealing with relatively small concerns and not huge companies like the pulp mills—that you can't calculate in advance. For instance, ideal winter logging conditions can glut the market so that you have to dump what you've already cut at giveaway prices (this happened to us twice), or you wake up one morning and find that the sawmill where you've been taking your logs has burned down during the night (this happened twice), or the mill operator, woeful, comes to tell you he has overextended his credit and can't pay for the logs you've already delivered, let alone be responsible for the ones you've got yarded in the woods and ready to go (this also happened two times), so you can never tell how a hardwood operation is going to turn out until the last log is delivered and paid for. You can lose your shirt or make a handsome packet.

During those first years we worked out what seemed to be a sustaining operation that could go on in an orderly thought-out way, indefinitely, and then on November 20, 1950, came the blowdown storm, and all our calculations and plans for controlled logging blew away with it—a great percentage of the balsam on the tract was an horrendous jungle of fallen trees that had to be salvaged and marketed quickly or not at all.

So for two years we cut only down-timber—a tedious exasperating chore—but we got 3100 cords before the remainder rotted beyond use.

After that we resumed normal cutting for three years, until another catastrophe developed—a massive infestation of blister rust got into the white pine in certain areas and was killing it at the rate of about 10 per cent each year, so there was nothing to do but clear-cut the whole stand of two million board feet. We had already cut the balsam from these areas, so when the pine was gone, they were dreary, inhospitable places that were offensive to look at and despicable to walk through. But that was twelve years ago. Today the young stand of evergreens is well over your head and growing like Topsy.

Since then, we have been able to do what we wanted, and not what we *had* to do—cutting as much or as little each year as we wished, or none at all.

We have logged off about one half of the tract. Today we can go back where we were twenty-five years ago and make another successful cut, not so grandiose surely, but remunerative, both financially and ecologically.

And then there is the other half of the tract—the outlying northerly areas stretching from Middle Beaver to Splitrock and Peaked Mountain and up the west slopes of Beaver Mountain —we are determined to keep it as the "forever wild" part of it—a great area that we will leave alone. It is mostly a forest of venerable hardwoods—seamy cat-faced old birches, and hard maples that are going bad at the stump and have knotholes at the top wherein there are undoubtedly thriving colonies of wood mice; and huge beeches with bear-claw marks on the bark that were inflicted a hundred years ago; and wolf-tree elms that shade half an acre of forest floor. No ecologist, no forester, no economist, could give you a practical reason for letting that woodland remain the way it is, but that's the way it's going to stay so long as we can keep it that way.

3.

One May day in 1966, I saw a small animal on the road in front of my house—it was dirty gray in color and the size of a

largish kitten. At first I thought this was what it must be even though all the clearing cats, both male and female, have been altered.

It paid me no attention as I came closer. It just walked aimlessly about the road on fumbling feet. It was definitely not a cat—it had the head of a fox and fox ears—but it wasn't a red fox or a cross, which are the only kinds on the tract of which we have any record.

I talked to it, trying to get its confidence, but it was suspicious, so I took off my windbreaker to use as a net, then I crowded it off the road into the blueberry brush and captured it. It struggled a bit, then became passive, and I took it out of the windbreaker to examine it. I was sitting there cross-legged in the brush, holding the little thing in my lap, and had got so far as to discover that it smelled slightly skunky and was a female, when suddenly she whipped her head down and snapped her canines, sharp as tacks, through my jeans and onto my shin. I concluded in somewhat less time than instantly, that my examination had progressed far enough and released her forthwith. She stumbled off through the brush and disappeared.

This animal was a gray fox, a cub that almost surely had become lost from its mother or been abandoned by her. Six months later, an adult was trapped two miles away, near Thumb Pond, so there is proof that still another new species of mammal has moved onto the Baker Tract.

In Squire Baker's time, the tract did not abound with quantities of diversified game. The climax virgin forest, omnipresent, provided a hospitable environment for only certain species of animals.

Baker and his various hired men were expert hunters and trappers, and their activities in these respects were largely confined to five species of animals—wolves, deer, mink, otters, and muskrats. Except for an occasional coon and bobcat, these were the only animals of which they, or Juliet Baker in her diary, left any record. There is no record of bears and none of beaver, nor is there any mention of fisher or pine marten or red foxes, or, strangest of all, snowshoe hares. Surely the men wouldn't

climax stand of decadent hardwoods.

have passed up any of these valuable animals had they been available, so they must have been extremely rare or totally absent.

The situation began to change almost immediately after Baker's arrival, and the transformation has been going on ever since. Today all the animals mentioned above—except for the wolves, which vanished forever from the tract in the late '60s —are at least as numerous as they were in Baker's time and, in most cases, far more numerous. With many species, this situation is due to the logging that has gone on over the years, and to natural catastrophes—the forest fire in 1867, another forty years later, then in 1950 the blowdown storm. All of these happenings leveled considerable sections of the climax forest, let in the sun that induced new growth within reach of the herbivorous animals, and the carnivorous predators naturally followed. It is not happenstance that the four animals which seem to be in more or less the same numbers today as they were a hundred years ago—otters, mink, muskrats, and coons—are primarily dependent on the streams and ponds and rivers, not the forest, for their food.

Deer responded to the changing environment, but it was a slow process at first—perhaps due to a dearth of breeding stock, perhaps because they were mercilessly hunted—and as late as 1895, when the State Conservation Commission was trying to put through a game law that would prohibit the hounding of deer, Rob Bibby, who was then the clearing boss, reported, "It is few deer they will get without dogs."

At the time Bibby wrote this, he was in the process of cutting the last stands of virgin pine and spruce on the tract (today there is just one such pine, on Nate Brook, that he failed to cut), and other lumbermen had conducted similar operations in the surrounding areas. Most of this timbering was in low-lying areas and around the pond shores—the natural wintering places for deer—and they flourished on the new growth. Since that time, there has been no dearth of them on the Baker Tract, but a curious interrelationship has developed, in respect to deer, between the tract and the thousands of acres of wilderness which surround it. Until 1885 the whole area was either privately owned or not claimed by anybody and was subjected impartially to the same logging treatment—and to the same natural disasters —so that the environment for deer was the same throughout. But in 1885 the areas surrounding the tract became part of the state-owned Forest Preserve and has since then been sacrosanct from logging, whereas the Baker Tract has been logged extensively and almost continuously.

Circa 1876—Splitrock Pond, some years after the great fire of 1867. Beneath the standing dead trees the young growth is coming up, and shortly after this picture was taken beaver returned to the pond and deer started to multiply.

Today there are far too many deer on the tract either for their own good or for the good of hardwood reproduction. They eat down the good available winter browse in the yarding areas much faster than it can grow back, so that they presently exist on barely subsistent food such as balsam and white pine. Not only this; they are so numerous that when they can move out of the wintering areas to the hardwood slopes, they eat back almost completely any reproduction of desirable species of hardwoods. This is because their favorite tree browse is yellow birch, maple, ash, and cherry—the most valuable species to a forest owner—and abhor beech to the extent that they will eat it only under starvation circumstances. (Foresters take an equally dim view of beech due to the poor quality of its lumber.) The result—all the hardwood areas on the Baker Tract are growing up exclusively to beech.

Under these circumstances, why do the deer not only stick to the tract but gravitate to it from the surrounding Forest Preserve? Why don't they go elsewhere? There are various factors which, put together, give the answer. For one, deer are relatively sedentary—five miles would be a very long distance for a deer to travel from summering grounds to a winter yarding area, and some Baker Tract deer, perhaps most of them, establish a home base in a certain yarding place and operate from there the year round. Another, and perhaps the most important factor, is that the critical time for deer comes in winter and early spring. If they can subsist during that time of deep snow, horrendous cold, and scant fare, they can flourish thereafter—no deer on the tract ever starved or lacked for decent food in summer and autumn. So deer stay on the tract, and many are enticed to it from the surrounding Forest Preserve lands, because there are at least survival circumstances during the bitter months (if they aren't too long and too severe), whereas the winter browse on the adjacent Preserve, where there has been no logging for seventy-five years, has long since been cropped off or has grown out of reach, so that there is no food, good or bad, at all. These areas constitute a slum-poverty situation for deer that is just as bad as the suffocating evergreen wilderness of Squire Baker's time.

Right now, and because of their excessive numbers, the deer on the tract are in a precarious situation. A hard winter, one that kept them locked in the yards from December to April, would decimate them. There hasn't been such a one since 1948.

Beech dominates the young hardwood growth.

Summer browse.

The winter of 1959–60 was moderately severe, but we saved countless deer by cutting browse for them. It was an act of mercy but an aggravation to the long-range problem—so that the population has been building up steadily to make an increasingly disparate relationship between the number of deer and the amount of available food. There are two solutions to this inevitably disastrous situation—we can remove the surplus by some means or let nature take its course.

The history of the Baker Tract beaver has been closely parallel to that of the deer. They benefited from every natural disaster —especially the fires—and from every logging operation that opened up the stream and pond shores to new growth. But beaver, even more than deer, are limited the year round in their radius of feeding action—a beaver rarely goes fifty yards from water to get food and hates to go even that far—and, unlike deer, they destroy a huge amount of tree growth in proportion to the food they get from it, so that they can soon exhaust a food supply, especially in ponds that they themselves have created, and be forced to vacate or live on inferior rations. So, even more than the deer, they have to be controlled if they are to survive.

Why there were few if any bears on the tract a hundred years ago, and why they began to show a marked increase about 1940, isn't readily explained, because it isn't a unique situation; it prevails in most sections of the Adirondacks. Surely the extensive hardwood logging operations that began in the 1930s on private

This buck has larger-than-average antlers, but he is runty in size. Although it is late June, he is still frowzy and emaciated from the winter ordeal.

The pond at the High Beaver Dam: everything in sight is dead—except the beaver. Left to proliferate, they would soon drown all vegetation within their reach and vacate.

lands, opening great areas to raspberry and blueberry growth, had something to do with it. Bears are the only mammal, other than some small rodents, that aren't remotely concerned about food during the cold months, so the relative prevalence of warm-weather edibles can influence their choice of environment far more than it does deer, for instance, whose first consideration is winter survival. This would explain why there has been a bear increase in certain areas, but it doesn't explain the over-all increase in numbers. Bears aren't prolific—a she-bear that produces one or two cubs every other year is doing her best—and the number of hunters has more than tripled since 1940, so you'd think that bears would be struggling for survival, but they aren't.

I think the reason is clear—there are three dependable and efficacious ways, all of them known to and practiced by the frontier hunters, to take bears. They can be bayed by hounds, or trapped, or lured to a bait in springtime and shot. The present-day conservation laws of the state rightly prohibit all of these practices so the hoard of present-day hunters, dependent on circumstantial and fortuitous meetings, can kill only an occasional unlucky one.

The abundance of red foxes and snowshoe hares on the tract is a cyclical thing and possibly interrelated. Some years there is a quantity of both, then they will disappear almost entirely. Both have been influenced by the logging operations and the natural disasters, but not as much as the deer and the beaver. The hares live impartially in either the new dense evergreen growth or in the old stagnant spruce and tamarack thickets, and the foxes, although preferring the clearings and other open places, can find mice and squirrels and chipmunks almost anywhere.

Foxes like the cut-over places.

It is probable that the fisher and pine marten had been trapped almost to extinction by the time Baker arrived on the tract, because they were prevalent throughout the virgin forests before that time. Both animals thrive on red squirrels and in addition will eat any meat they can kill, or find dead, so both can exist comfortably in forests that haven't been lumbered or otherwise disturbed.

For many years fisher were a rarity on the tract and pine marten were assumed to be extinct. In 1921 a man shot a fisher, and the carcass had to be sent to the conservation department to be identified. They continued to be scarce until the 1940s, when they began to increase, and they have been proliferating ever since, so that it is now not at all unusual to see one.

My first awareness that marten had returned to the tract was in November 1955, when I found their tracks in the snow, lacing through a spruce thicket on Peaked Mountain. The following winter, when I was camped on Splitrock, I came across their tracks constantly. And three years ago there was ample evidence that they were living, at least temporarily, in the Mink Pond swamp, about a quarter of a mile from my house. They are almost entirely nocturnal, and the only one I've seen was a small, light-colored thing, flitting like a banshee through the spruce tops, just before dark.

The return of fisher and marten to the tract, and to other remote areas of the Adirondacks, is reasonable. Under state protection, and with few competent trappers to scourge them, they have simply reinhabited the terrains which naturally suit them.

Otters and mink have times of abundance and scarcity on the tract, which may be cyclical or may be caused haphazardly by disease. It certainly isn't caused by a relative abundance of food, because the supply for both animals—small frogs, polliwogs, minnows, crayfish, and occasionally small trout (these animals on the tract are not the awful trout killers they are reputed elsewhere to be)—remains constant year after year. Whatever causes the rise and fall in their numbers, it seems to affect both animals at the same time. In the summer of 1965, for instance, both were abundant—one day on Mink and Thumb

Skulls—from left, bear, coyote, beaver, bobcat, otter, and mink.

Ponds I saw seventeen otters in family groups of seven, six, and four, and signs of a big mink population were everywhere. The following year, I saw two otters in early April and not another one after that, and mink were scarce all summer and fall.

The number of muskrats on the tract remains fairly static—they are never plentiful and never scarce, but there are at least a few everywhere there is water—on the river, streams, ponds, and beaver flows. Something seems to happen to a number of them every winter. They either suffocate under the ice or get icebound so that they starve or freeze to death, or the young get drowned in their dens by the rising water—at any rate there are always more in the autumn than in early spring.

I doubt that there has ever been a dearth of coons on the tract except during those times when some sort of disease strikes them, which it not infrequently does. A great deal of a coon's fare comes from the water's edge and, like his cousin, the bear, he isn't particularly concerned about a winter food supply—he can go to sleep when it is unobtainable and forage again when times are propitious—so he is seldom in distress.

Coons sometimes reach plague proportions on the tract. I say "plague" because when they reach these numbers they are not only an abomination about the clearing but also are frightful depredators of all ground-nesting birds, especially ducks. Invariably, after such a coon surfeit, they die off and, in my experience this is apt to happen in April, after they emerge from their dens.

Within my memory, at least four species of mammals have become newly established on the tract—the gray foxes already mentioned, gray squirrels, coyotes, and a strange breed of woodchuck.

The squirrels were first noted in 1929, when a small colony was discovered on a beech ridge near Splitrock Pond—it is still there—and subsequently four more colonies, each one isolated from the others and invariably in beech woods, have come into being. Their existence is precarious. The numbers in the individual colonies never seem to increase. This is because winter survival is a touch-and-go thing with them—unlike red squirrels, which can thrive on a diet of evergreen cones; gray squirrels depend on such food as beechnuts and maple seeds that lie under the deep snow. And there is another factor which hinders their increase—living as they do in open hardwoods, they are a fat target for the goshawks and horned owls which favor the same habitat. It is something of a miracle that the squirrels survive.

The coyotes, or brush wolves, arrived in New York State from Canada in the 1930s and were first noticed on the Baker Tract in the summer of 1948. They have been there, in fluctuating numbers, ever since, much to the consternation of some people and the delight of others. It was greatly feared at first that they would decimate the deer, but they haven't, and there is no present indication that they ever will. It is certain that they kill some deer, mostly in early spring, when the snow is deep and the deer emaciated, but mostly they seem to be very high on rabbits, and are ardent mousers, and are partial to any kind of carrion, and fruit in season, so that their appetite is similar to that of red foxes.

These animals are a large species of coyote—the largest dead male I've seen weighed forty-eight pounds, the largest female, thirty-eight.

I doubt they would have settled permanently on the tract if it hadn't been for our logging operations. Again like red foxes, they favor open sunny knolls, and clearings, and old blueberry "burns," and beaver meadows, and they make great use of log roads and skid paths and trails. Basically, they aren't a deep woods animal.

I think there are presently two, and possibly three, family groups—adults, yearlings, and puppies—that range the length and breadth of the tract, and far beyond. Whether the families have clear-cut individual territories I don't know. I think they must at least overlap.

The coyotes have not increased greatly on the tract in the last ten years. If anything, they have slightly declined. About

Coyote—probably about a year and a half old.

seven years ago they became afflicted with a mange named scabies mite that ravaged them so that for a time they almost disappeared from the tract. Now they are making a slow comeback.

There is some doubt as to whether the woodchucks that began to show up on the tract and in other sections of the Adirondacks about ten years ago are a species unlike the common or garden variety found on open farmlands, or merely a strain of that animal. At any rate they don't look like the farm woodchuck, except in general conformation, and they don't act like it. These animals are smaller and grizzly dark gray, sometimes almost black, and they do indeed inhabit the woods, apparently from preference, because they live around and about the clearing, but not *on* it. Their preference seems to be for open hardwoods and, in some peculiar instances, watery places. I know of three different sets of them that are presently living in culverts on our road, and they get a soaking every time it rains. Furthermore they are good tree climbers, but that isn't unusual with ordinary woodchucks.

I don't know from whence they came or what prompted them to take up permanent residence on the tract, but that apparently is their intention.

There are some animals which are not now, and to my knowledge never have been, on the tract, at least in my time, but whose arrival wouldn't be cause for much surprise. Possums, for instance—they have been extending their range northward for some years—and last autumn I saw one dead on the highway, about twenty airline miles to the south of the tract. And cottontail rabbits—they abound not far away too. And skunks—they are prevalent in some sections of the Adirondacks, but, for some inexplicable reason, not ours—yet. And lynx—for years they were thought to be extinct in the Adirondacks, but a few years ago one was shot about twenty-five miles east of the Baker Tract, and there may be more about. (It is also conceivable they could migrate south from Canada, as the coyotes did.) And moose—just before Baker's arrival on the tract they were numerous throughout the Adirondacks (reports indicate that in some areas they were more prevalent than deer), and presently they are increasing in Maine, New Brunswick, and New Hampshire, not far away.

One animal I would most like to see on the tract and which I never will—unless it is imported—is the mountain lion. It is a curious thing about them—over a century ago they frequented the Adirondacks, surely in no great numbers, and despite the fact that the last authenticated killing of one occurred in 1894,

Trapping in the Beaver Ponds area. There is nothing but alder, hazel brush, tamarack, and spruce here—a poverty situation for beaver—so they have to be drastically controlled.

there are many people who persist in the belief that they are still about, and I know a few men who will vow on the Bible that they have seen one. They haven't, more's the pity.

In accounting for the abundance and variety of game on the tract today, as opposed to its relative scarcity a hundred years ago, I have put stress on logging operations and natural disasters which have disrupted the orderly scheme of the wilderness in much the same way that new forces invade an entrenched civilization and reinvigorate it. But there are other factors which made it possible.

For one thing, Squire Baker was but one of hundreds of frontiersmen throughout the Adirondacks who caught or killed anything that would give him subsistence—they were efficient and lethal operators—but there are no such professionals working full time at it today, and there are only a few who can do it on even a supplementary basis. Hunting has become largely an avocation of weekend amateurs who stay close to the roads and try to make up in numbers and temporary enthusiasm what they lack in skill and endurance; trapping is almost a bygone profession, not only because the remuneration is paltry but because the opportunity to learn the trade and the desire to become proficient have just about vanished.

Another consideration is that the State of New York has fairly stringent game laws—you can't, for instance, hound deer any more, or snare them, or jacklight them; it is illegal to hound or trap a bear; the beaver season is usually in early spring—the most difficult and arduous time to trap them; most other fur bearers are protected eight months of the year.

But the restrictions aren't all *that* severe. For instance, there is a one-buck-only law, but there are also provisions, where deer are too numerous, for a man to kill an additional deer of either sex; there is a special early bear season which was instituted in the hope that people would take to the woods and kill more bears (in practice, most interested hunters take to the town garbage dumps and hunt them there); there is no limit on the number of fur bearers, except for marten, that a man may trap, and there are almost no restrictions on how he may trap them, and the open season extends for the entire time that their skins are prime; there is no closed season at all on foxes, coyotes, and bobcats, and some Adirondack counties, pressured by misguided people, even pay bounties for dead coyotes and bobcats. The fact that these liberal provisions exist, and that the game in the *wilderness* areas continues to thrive and multiply in spite of them, would indicate that hunters and trappers are becoming less and less of an influence. There is a huge and widening gap between human civilization and the wilderness which ever-fewer men have the yen to penetrate or the ability to exploit.

Summer

1.

Adirondack people like to make jokes about the short duration of summer—standard quips go something like, "Summer was on a Thursday this year," or, "I just had time to wash my long johns before I had to put them back on again." Things like that. It's nonsense of course—we usually have three or four heat waves, and sometimes the hot dry weather lasts six weeks or more, but, unlike the other seasons, there's no precise change of mood that proclaims its arrival. Spring, for instance, starts the day the ice goes out of Mink Pond; autumn beings on Labor Day, when the children go home to school and a quiet settles over the clearing; winter comes with the first authoritative blizzard, but spring and summer merge gently so that it is some time before you are aware of the transition.

It hasn't got much to do with temperature or climate change, because there can be sultry heat in early May, a snowstorm in June, raw wet spells in July, and frosts in August. What sets summer, early summer, that is, apart from spring, is the difference between expectancy and fulfillment, between courtship and marriage.

For me, the realization of summer comes in a variety of ways.

The buck, Stupid, who last year was the darling of the clearing, and who was photographed as though he were Rin-Tin-Tin, and who learned nothing of caution during the hunting season, and who comes regularly to my salt licks—Stupid at long last has shed his frowzy winter hair and is thinly sleek and clean, and furthermore his antlers have suddenly burgeoned—they're well above his ears and he's going to have at least six tines, maybe eight.

And sitting on the porch of a still evening, watching the mist mushroom from the hidden ponds and the distant river, there comes from the west bay of Mink the sonorous booming of the bullfrogs—all is right with the world, and with each bullfrog, individually, and there isn't a thing to worry about.

And perhaps on the same night, or another soon after, there are fireflies winking shyly out there in the pasture, like nuns questing for a lost soul.

And there's the time, just after sundown, that you slide up in a canoe to the beaver house in the west bay of Mink, and float for a while until, from inside the house there comes a mewing singsong whimpering, like baby puppies, and you know that there's a healthy, hungry litter in there. And if you wait long enough—a couple of minutes—and are quiet enough, there comes a plop sound from within, then a string of bubbles comes up outside the house, then a parent beaver surfaces and starts on a foraging expedition, or goes on a reconnoiter. (Parent beavers are as various in temperament and in their reactions to child-rearing as humans; there are placid beavers, and nervous types, and there are hysterical slap-happy ones that cruise about like Paul Reveres, trying to alert the pondside to all manner of imagined perils and extremities, to which absurd activity none of the other animals—the deer, loons, otters, muskrats, even the trout—pay the slightest heed.)

Paul Revere beaver.

About the tenth of June, new fawns begin to show up on the clearing and on the pond shores with their mothers, and it's something of a wonderful surprise to see them; you can't understand how the mothers, after all those months of cruel weather and near-starvation, can produce such chipper offspring. (Mother deer are as various in temperament and character as beavers; there are loving, patient mothers, and there are stingy irritable ones who seem to feel that giving milk to their young is like giving up the blood of life, and then there are the does, runty and bedraggled, that trail about with their offspring like beggars in a ghetto.)

And sometime late in June, there is an awareness that most of the birds have stopped singing—the love-making is over and now it's time for the down-to-earth business of child-rearing. Those male birds—most ducks and many songsters—who shun this drab aspect of family life, become silent and morosely aloof; the ones who take a more responsible view are far too busy to sing about it. So an occasional whitethroat or vireo or peewee, or late in the evening a hermit thrush, is about all you'll hear.

Tree swallows.

All of these things, taken together, mean that summer has come, and not long thereafter arrives what I think of as the dead of summer—it is the drabbest time of year because anything unexpected rarely happens, and almost everything is predictable.

For instance, you can predict that the brook trout in the various ponds will retire to deep water about July 15 and be-

Mink Pond—sundown.

come wholly unco-operative with fly fishermen so that only the most uncouth arrangement of bait and orchestrated hardware will tempt an occasional one.

The steers, heifers, and bull, which heretofore have been content with the forage in the pasture, now find that it has dried up and not at all to their liking; as a consequence, they break through the fence and take to the greener woods to meander with infuriating unconcern. (A few years ago during a heat wave and dry spell, they set off on such a junket and it took us four days to find them; they were amusing themselves in the river, miles away. We got the steers and heifers back to the clearing all right, but the bull was recalcitrant, so we left him. Three days later he showed up, disgusted, fagged out, and wholly dehydrated by his return trip through the parched woods. He drank the watering trough nearly dry, then lay down and didn't budge for two days, which was fine with us.)

In August, predictably, the logging operation, which normally is the cleanest outdoor work there is, turns into a filthy labor; the horses become impatient and miserable from the heat and the deer flies; sweat and dust and softwood pitch combine to cake you with black sticky grime that only kerosene can remove;

the sun takes forever to go down; that bottle of beer at nightfall is too good to be true—August logging can be purely hell.

Predictably, the dead of summer brings an ennui that comes from the feeling and knowledge that things are going to get worse before they get better; the woods will get drier, the weather more sultry, the swallows will go away and after them most of the songbirds—for a long time there will be a hiatus of sound and activity. At such times, my inclination is to be abroad at dawn and home again before the inertia of heat sets in, stay there until the sun goes down and the persistent wind abates, then paddle about one of the ponds to see what's going on, most especially with the deer. (It's an interesting thing about deer—on dry land they are apt to be highly nervous and give the impression that they are living on borrowed time and don't get any pleasure from life, but when in or close to water, undisturbed, they become absorbed in languid pleasure. Maybe just being in the environment of water puts animals at a certain ease; water animals such as beavers, otters, muskrats, and even frogs seem more relaxed and confident than land animals, and I never saw any one of them going anywhere with compulsive speed or psychotic preoccupation for its own safety.)

Doe and American mergansers.

At such a time, you don't even have to summon the energy that will get you to a pond; you can sit on the porch and watch the sunset. August produces the very finest sort because the heat of the day builds up towering masses of cumulus in the western sky that hulk over the mountains and soak up, and refract, the ever-changing light. As the light and wind diminish, there comes a fine hush and the only sound is the murmurous tinkling of the cowbells, way up in the far end of the pasture. And then, just before total dark, there are vague scratching noises from the attic overhead, and the flying squirrels scramble out through the hole under the eaves, climb to the peak of the roof, and arc off like black saucers into the balsam swamp.

The dead of summer isn't quite as bad as I make it out to be.

2.

About the tenth of June the clearing does—those that habituate the place and are semitame—show up with their new off-spring, and it's exciting and gratifying to see each arrival. The mothers, or most of them anyway, we know well, and each has a distinctive personality. There is Pauline, for instance, who for

six years in a row has produced fine healthy twins and always takes wonderful care of them, and then there is Mossy—the self-appointed queen of the clearing—who is a mean cantankerous old bag who loathes child-rearing but annually produces a nervous unhappy offspring which she tries, as much as possible, to keep out of sight and mind.

I have read a great deal about the ritual that mother deer are supposed to go through when having their fawns—how, when the time is imminent, they retire to some sequestered place, shunning all other deer and most especially the bucks, and hide the fawn, and introduce it only very carefully to the outside world. All this sounds right, and maybe it is right in most instances, but I wonder how many people have actually been a witness under natural circumstances.

I wonder this because one spring day a few years ago, I was involved in a two-day cliff-hanger sequence that confounded all my ideas on the subject.

Mossy.

It happened this way: all spring long, while sitting in my high big-windowed office that is like a watchtower, I had been keeping close track on the deer that frequented my end of the clearing and which came to my salt licks, and in doing so I became acquainted with a measly two-year-old doe, much emaciated and woebegone from the winter, which was one of Mossy's miserable children. I used to speculate as to whether or not she was pregnant (it is sometimes impossible to know this just from looking at a deer) and had more or less concluded that she was not, possibly because I *hoped* she wasn't (I wasn't too keen on having her bloodline perpetuated). Then one cold rainy morning—June 9—she came ambling up from the swamp, passed the salt licks without stopping, and meandered onto my "lawn." She was trailing afterbirth.

A few minutes later, I saw something else coming up from the swamp. I thought at first it was a young fox (foxes and coyotes have a passion for afterbirth of any sort), but no, it was a fawn, the very smallest that I've ever seen. It was making torturous stumbling headway through the blueberry bushes, but when it finally got on the lawn, it caught up with its mother, and it was then that I saw its umbilical cord.

They went out of sight in the dip of the clearing by the alder tangle, and then, a few minutes later, the doe, feeding, appeared on the far side of the dip. Then I saw the fawn; it had left its mother and was returning the way it had come. It came onto the lawn and lay down right in the middle of it, not twenty feet from my house.

I watched the mother, feeding with unconcern way over there in the pasture, then I went to get the clearing boss to come and confirm that this fawn was, in fact, incredibly minute. He came, agreed that it was, and thereafter was as concerned with its welfare as I. We didn't touch the thing, in fact approached no nearer than fifteen feet of it, and the mother, over in the pasture, never bothered to look in our direction.

We went upstairs to my watchtower and waited, hoping to see the doe come for its child, but she finally went into the woods and we saw her no more that day.

The fawn huddled on the lawn in a ball so small it would literally have fitted into a pie plate; even from upstairs, looking down into the short grass, it was almost impossible to see it. It stayed that way, as if it were in a deep sleep, all day, and when night came it was still there.

I worried about it; the rain had turned to spitting snow, and here was this frail thing lying wholly exposed. However could it survive? I went to bed assuring myself that the mother would come for it and all would be well.

The next morning, I couldn't see it from the office window, but, just to make sure, I went out. By golly, it was still there, curled up and flat to the ground, just as it had been the evening before.

I spent an uneasy and unfruitful morning in the office, keeping vigilance. Various deer, including old Mossy and a spikehorn buck, browsed about and visited the licks, but the mother was strangely absent.

And then, about one o'clock, she appeared from the woods. She was quartering back and forth, searching, and as she came

Spikehorn, Silly, and Mossy.

close to the lawn, some queer confounding things took place. First, she encountered that old harridan, her mother, and made a swift, determined hoof-striking lunge at her, and old Mossy retreated in dismay. Then the spikehorn approached and the young doe made a similar lunge at him, but he stood his ground, and thereafter they were wholly compatible; he followed her about and seemed to be as concerned as she was in her quest. Mossy, the while, stayed at a distance and watched the proceedings with the keenest interest, but took no active part in them.

The young doe and the spikehorn couldn't find the fawn. They quartered about the lawn like slow bird dogs and sometimes came within a few feet of the tiny thing, then they probed around the pasture and down to the swamp, then came back to the lawn again. I got more and more exasperated, I kept wanting to shout at them or give hand signals, or something, and every time they got close to the fawn I held my breath, sensing that we might be about to win the game.

It was the buck, by sheer inadvertence, that finally found it by almost stepping on it. He put his nose down to whiff, and reacted as if he'd come on a rattlesnake—he snorted and catapulted away, and the doe went with him.

They stopped out in the clearing and stood a moment—as if considering the fact that they'd made fools of themselves—then they came back, leery, sniffing their way as though they were going through a minefield. The doe (I had named her Silly by this time) approached her offspring, looked aghast at it, put her nose down for a smell, and reacted as the buck had done—she snorted, and they raced away.

Silly.

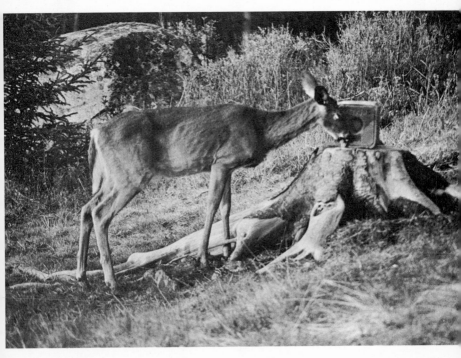

Thereafter, they ignored the fawn; they browsed about, licked long and with absorption on the salt, and finally went away together into the swamp.

It was a case of blatant abandonment. I became ever more sure of this as the afternoon wore on and the doe didn't come out of the swamp, and more convinced too that if the fawn were to survive it would have to have foster parents, namely the boss and myself. I went to get him.

Later, still loath to interfere, we were sitting at the window trying to piece together what little either of us knew about baby formulas, when suddenly there on the edge of the lawn in the half-dark was Silly. She was looking toward her fawn and for a long time she just stood there, then she must have made a sound that we couldn't hear through the closed windows, because suddenly the fawn sprang up, raced to her, and made a bumbling effort to nurse. And then again suddenly—as if she had just become aware of the need to be secretive—Silly bounded off to the swamp, the fawn following, and when we saw them last, the fawn was having no trouble keeping the pace.

We pondered the reactions of four deer to fawn birth—Silly, who neglected her offspring, and then couldn't find it, and behaved so strangely thereafter; the fawn itself, which left its mother and bedded down of its own volition with what, in retrospect, appears to have been unconcern. And after huddling there for thirty-some hours without moving until told to do so, responded with vigor. What about that? And old Mossy, the dowager of the clearing, who was cowed by her own daughter and strangely intrigued by the subsequent search? And finally the spikehorn, who couldn't possibly have had a paternal interest, but was accepted and trusted by Silly, and assisted as best he knew how? And why the horror of both Silly and the buck at finding what she was looking for?

I think we may have come up with an idea that explains a good deal about Silly; at the time this incident was transpiring, she possibly hadn't started to lactate and, being a first-time mother, was bewildered and irresponsible; when finally the milk came down, the maternal instinct developed.

We concluded nothing about the fawn; what it did must have been pure instinct, but nonetheless its patience and self-control were nothing short of miraculous—babies, of any kind, are just not supposed to be like that.

As for the buck and Mossy, their conduct confounded everything that either of us had ever seen or heard or read—the buck should have been off somewhere with a crony, or else in aloof solitude, and Mossy should have been nagging her own new and despised offspring, or else maintaining her status as Number One in the peck order of the clearing deer. What bewitched them?

Silly and her fawn were about the clearing all summer and fall. The fawn remained pathetically small, never grew a healthy coat of winter hair, and disappeared about the end of November. Silly survived the winter, just barely, and produced another in June.

3.

A loon is something more than a bird—it is a creature that would have fascinated Edgar Allan Poe if he had ever encountered one, or heard one, which I doubt that he did. They are the evocation of the northern wilds.

Yearly and without fail and for as long as I can remember, there has been a pair of mated loons on Mink Pond. I say "a pair," which suggests that it's the same pair every year, but I don't know this, and it's probably not so, but I like to think it. I like to think that the same birds come back year after year. It is possible that this is so, because their routine and basic conduct never vary; they arrive the day after the ice goes out of Mink and they leave together, no matter what the weather conditions might be, on or about October 18; in spring, before egg incubation and child-rearing starts, they invariably take off from the pond in late afternoon, calling to each other, and fly away for the night, then just after dawn they come back from wherever they've been, calling again (it's a fine alarm clock); when they've settled down to the business of raising a family, only one bird takes off on these overnight junkets, and when it flies back again at sunup, screaming protestations of good faith, it is answered by sonorous melancholic complaint from its for-

saken mate on the pond; surely they must be long-married and have an understanding. Or so I like to think.

But this is sentimentality—I have impressions and supposi-tions about the Mink loons, but few facts. For instance, how do they know, precisely, when the ice is out of the pond? What are these overnight trips all about? Is it to keep in flight training, or do they go somewhere with a purpose in mind, such as fishing, or is it an aimless compulsion to wander? When child-raising starts and it is imperative that one bird stay at home, which one is it that takes off at night and returns at dawn—is it he, she, or each one alternately? When they're out there in the pond, diving and presumably fishing, what are they after—trout, little chubs or sunfish, crustacea, mussels, polli-wogs—what? And why are they so solitary? Why does only a single pair ever nest on the pond?

I don't know the answer to any of these things and I doubt that anyone does, because loons don't lend themselves to comprehensive study; they are loners in remote places, and their sex is cloaked in total similarity of appearance, and of all waterfowl they are perhaps the most difficult to "collect." (To know much about any animal, you have to collect and examine a great number of them. No one has ever done this with loons, and I doubt they will, and I hope they don't.)

I have killed one loon in my life, and I am not proud of it, but it came about this way. When I was about fifteen and had a lust for shooting things, a group of us at Baker's Clearing decided arbitrarily that the loons on Mink Pond were the primary cause of the poor trout fishing there, hence they must be done away with. An expedition was organized, and six boats and canoes, with men and boys rifled and shotgunned, sallied forth against a pair of sitting loons and their two young. Well, the cannonading was fierce, but every time we cornered one of the birds, it would dive just as we shot, and swim underwater and come up behind us, so that we had to ambush it somewhere else and try again. Finally, down in a narrow bay, we boxed in one of the immature birds, quite exhausted, and when it surfaced I shot it with a 44/40. A pretty story, but it partly explains why there has been no exhaustive study of loons and why so little, really, is known about them.

In my time, loons have nested on only two of the Baker Tract ponds—habitually on Mink and sporadically on Thumb. Both are trout ponds which also have a dense population of small coarse fish—pumpkinseeds, shiners, chubs, dace and bullheads —and also crayfish, fresh-water mussels, and green frogs and bullfrogs in all stages of development. So the loons have a varied bill of fare if they choose to partake of it, but my strong supposition is that they, and other loons, are so predilected to trout that they will eat them whenever they can get them. (I am speaking now of what loons eat in warm-weather times when they are living on inland fresh water; what they eat in winter when they're on the sea coast is a different kettle.) I think this for a number of reasons. For one, loons have a seeming abhorrence of shallow water and lily pads—where the small coarse fish and frogs are most apt to be—and stay in the deeper waters,

where the trout surely are. On a unique occasion a few years ago, I surprised the Mink loons in the narrow shallow neck of the inlet—they sensed that they were caught off base and reacted instantly—they dove and came down the neck like erratic torpedoes, flashed under the canoe, and made good their escape into deep water. Subsequently, I found out that there were small trout where they had been, and I presume that is why they were there, out of their accustomed depth.

Another reason to believe that loons are more than partial to trout is that they never nest on Splitrock Pond and rarely frequent it—but on the maps of a hundred years ago, Splitrock was named Loon Pond. That was when it was one of the finest trout ponds in the Adirondacks, and before some misguided person dumped bass in it, which eradicated the trout in short order. In the diary of Squire Baker's daughter, there is this entry, dated February 22, 1867: "Went a-fishing to Loon Pond, caught 22 pound." Pretty nice fishing, I'd say, and the loons must have thought so too, but they don't any more.

The only pond, other than Mink or Thumb, which they frequent with some regularity, is Frank, and they have been doing that for only four years—starting at precisely the time we rehabilitated it as a trout pond after first poisoning every other fish in it. So when I see a loon diving there with great

Circa 1875—a catch of trout from "Loon" Pond.

absorption, the assumption is overwhelming that it has trout in mind.

Loons don't nest on Frank because it is too small a body of water to assure their being able to take off whenever they choose—in their efforts to get airborne, they are not unlike those World War II 4-engine flying boats—they need an almost-inexhaustible water way, proper wind conditions, a bit of luck, and a small prayer. A few years ago, on a still afternoon, I was on Frank and became increasingly exasperated with a loon that was fishing out there and apparently catching more trout than I was, so I determined to rout it out. I pursued it about, slapping my paddle every time it surfaced, and finally had it in such a state of torment that it made a frenzied effort to quit the place—and it wasn't unlike Lindbergh taking off from Roosevelt Field for Paris—it was touch-and-go, hold-your-breath, all the way. It got barely airborne at the far end of the pond when, making a U-turn to come back, it stalled out and hit the water, and bounced up and was flying again. Four times it circled the pond, striving for the altitude that would get it above the trees and out of there, but it just plain couldn't— it finally gave up and made an ignominious crash landing. (It swam away from the disaster, however, which is what counts in an emergency.)

This incapacity for quick and short take-offs is a limiting factor as to where loons can abide, and perhaps their most deadly shortcoming. Last spring, when Minerva Creek was in spate and overflowing its banks, a pair of migrating loons alighted there—the water receded quickly and the loons, trapped, languished all summer, produced no young, and apparently never got out. And there was a time many years ago that a loon was discovered, incapacitated and miserable, in our upper pasture —it had set down there on a foggy night, mistaking the pasture for water, and was instantly helpless. It was taken to Mink Pond, and it swam away, and no one knows what happened to it.

Loons have an abhorrence of land because they can barely stagger along, and the only time they willingly come onto it is to nest. Even then, they go the minimum distance necessary, sometimes a mere few inches, rarely more than two feet, and so precarious is the nesting situation that a slight rise of the water level will drown the eggs. I've seen this happen twice.

The nests, at least the ones I've seen, aren't nests at all; they're just nesting *places,* on grass or even on bare gravel, and sometimes with no effort at concealment, so that the eggs are an open and succulent invitation to any and every predator, especially coons. I am sure that the main reason the Mink Pond loons successfully hatch young, more often than not, is that they invariably nest on one of the islands, away from most of the four-footed predators.

Loons make a variety of cries and calls and sounds; there is that high-pitched, far-reaching cackle of unfunny laughter that gives them their name. And there is that wailing grievous call that is as eerie and sad as the complaint of a lone coyote. I am sure that this is the effort of one bird to contact its mate, because last summer one of the Mink loons went on a foray to Thumb—a scant hundred yards away—and got stranded there, due either to wind conditions or molt, and for two weeks, night and day, the two wailed back and forth to each other.

There is a third, scarcely audible sound they make when a pair is close together—a low, confidential mewing sort of whisper. It sounds like love talk to me.

And there is still a fourth noise, which I doubt many people know about, that pierces out when the bird is in a hysterical frenzy of rage. I have heard this only once, and it was under weird and incomprehensible circumstances.

It came about this way. In the spring and summer of 1965, the Mink loons apparently failed to hatch any young, and were behaving like any childless parents who have nothing better to do than gad about—they were forever leaving the pond and coming back. Then, on July 13, I saw three loons on the pond, together, and I surmised that one of them must be a child that I hadn't known about.

The next day, driving by the pond on my way to town for supplies, I saw a loon in the lily pads by the outlet. This in itself was strange due to a loon's aversion to shallow water, but it was also behaving peculiarly; it paid no attention to me although I was close by, and it seemed dowdy and lethargic, not sleek and alert as a loon usually is, and it tried many times to rise up in the water to beat its wings, but couldn't do it. I presumed it was sick, so I put out in a canoe to see what I could discover about it.

It swam slowly and rather aimlessly, keeping just ahead of me and staying in the lily pads. Sometimes it dove and swam underwater, but it couldn't stay down for more than a few seconds.

At this point, two loons on the far side of the pond started swimming toward us, screaming as they came. I instantly assumed that the bird in front of me, albeit of good size, was their separated offspring, so I maneuvered the canoe to herd it out into the pond, and so reunite the family.

While I did this, the pair was coming forward fast, shrieking mightily—which I took to be an indication of parental hysteria, but which wasn't, and when they were about a hundred yards away, I turned back to shore, quite smug in the assumption that I'd done my good deed for the day.

I had no sooner beached the canoe than a great commotion erupted on the pond—it was too far away to see what was going on, but there was no doubt that a no-holds-barred fight between two of the birds was taking place, and I naturally assumed that two males were contesting for the lady. I scrambled back into the canoe and hurried out.

At first, I was careful not to approach too close lest I break up this encounter, so I stayed at a distance and watched a frightful, vicious, ruthless incident.

It was now obvious that these birds had had a previous fight and that the one I had been concerned about had been decisively whipped; what was going on now was like a KO'd prize fighter being made to stand up again to Sonny Liston.

It was a no-contest fight from the beginning—the dominant bird would stab at its opponent, just behind the head, and hold on, then quite deliberately flail it on the chest with the elbow of its wing, blow after blow, then, tiring of this, it would slam the victim's head underwater and hold it down; then suddenly it would dive, dragging the other bird with it, and for as much as twenty seconds they'd be down there out of sight, with nothing but some bubbles coming up; then they'd come flailing to the surface, and the whole grisly sequence would start over again; and while this was going on, the third bird swam close by, shrieking with maniacal ecstasy, like a French lunatic at Marat's execution.

There was no need for caution on my part—if the birds were not oblivious of my presence, they were surely unmindful of it—and I came so close that once, when the murderer dragged its victim underwater, they came up on the other side of the canoe, a mere paddle length away.

It went on for an eternity, a half hour perhaps, and then finally I thought it was over; after one of those underwater treatments, the victor came bursting to the surface, rose up to beat its wings, and crowed like Cassius Clay; then the other bird came floating to the top and lay there, belly-up, with its great black feet wanly flapping in the air, like an old old drunk trying to wipe away flies.

But it wasn't over—the bird righted itself, and its bill came out of water, and it slumped there, sick unto death but still alive. The victor was enraged; from twenty feet away it plunged underwater and erupted on it from below, and once again the assault was on.

Three times it left that bird for dead. Twice it came back to complete what it had failed to do. And then the thing was lying there in the water, inert, and I picked it up and started for shore.

But there was still life in it; it sprawled on the bottom of the canoe, legs and wings limp, but its eyes were alive. When I got to shore, its head was up.

I put it under a bank in shallow water, and left it.

When I went back a few hours later, it was alive.

Sometime after that, when I returned with a friend, it was dead.

I delivered the corpse for autopsy to a friend of mine who is a research investigator for the state conservation department.

His report, coming a week later, was a real bomb; the bird which I had assumed to be a male was, in fact, an adult female.

This gives rise to some fascinating speculation that can never be resolved. What was the sex of the killer bird? Was the dead bird an interloper on the pond, or vice versa? What caused the fight at a time of year—midsummer—when sexual motivations are normally at an end?

There was another bit of interesting, and possibly pertinent, information, in the report; although the dead bird was fat and in excellent condition, there was in its stomach a large much eroded lead fishing sinker, attached to a two-foot length of nylon leader. The lead, stated the report, would surely have poisoned it eventually.

There was an odd sequel; two days after the battle I was on Mink with a friend, when we came upon three adult loons —they were together, and apparently, most companionable. The war—what war? Whose war? Why?—had been put out of mind, and everything was serene and innocent, as if nothing had happened.

4.

In the dead of summer there comes a Sunday, or two at the most, which provides a most salubrious occasion to go bobber-fishing for pike on Lower Beaver Pond.

This requires explanation. To begin, there is a certain idiocy in fishing for pike there at all—(the Random House dictionary defines "idiocy" as "utterly senseless or foolish behavior")—because a fish that you catch in those warm, mucky sphagnum depths is flatulent, slimy, foul-smelling, and abhorrent to the taste, so that as soon as you get him in the boat you are overcome with disgust for him, and for yourself for having occasioned the uncouth situation. So if you're going to engage in this practice at all, it's got to be on the seventh day, when you have at least a biblical right to "rest" in any manner that suits you, so long as it isn't morally offensive, and it cannot be on a weekday when you've simply got to have something to show, however inferior, for your labors. So a Sunday it has to be, but not just any Sunday; it has to be a quiet overcast Sunday because a day of hot dry sun or persistent wind will disrupt the euphoric purpose of the expedition. (Again, Random House defines "euphoria" as "a feeling of well-being, esp. an exaggerated one having no basis in truth or reality.") It has to be a Sunday when Lower Beaver Pond reflects every activity, however slight, that disturbs its surface—a damsel fly dipping its eggs into the water, or a barn swallow kissing down, or, most especially, the slightest movement of your bobber. Such a Sunday comes once or twice each summer.

The expedition cannot be planned long in advance—it has to be a fortuitous happening that combines mellifluous weather circumstances with your state of whimsey—but you can make tentative preparations for it in the same way that our joint chiefs-of-staff take into consideration any eventuality—be it in China, or Santo Domingo or Paris, France—that might arise. For instance, there should be a supply of chubs in the bait box at Mink Pond, and all the deadly equipment for the foray should be stock-piled and immediately at hand, and, most important of all, you must have an ally in the venture upon whose simpletonian pleasures and zeal you can rely as faithfully as you can your own.

About this ally—he absolutely cannot be anyone who is eager to catch a pike in hot weather in a stagnant sphagnum pond; he must be fully aware that to do such a monstrous thing implies various pursuant disagreeable circumstances, to wit: 1) it disrupts the serenity of the venture, which is your sole objective;

2) it entails cleaning and dressing the misbegotten thing, and 3) it finally creates a choice of three miserable alternatives: do you boil it up and make a pretense of eating the horror, or do you present it to someone you don't like and would prefer not to see again, or do you offer it to the cat, who would be sure to take umbrage? (Random House defines "umbrage" as "offense, annoyance, displeasure; to feel umbrage at a social snub . . . to take umbrage at somone's rudeness.") The truth is that there is no satisfactory way to dispose of a dead Lower Beaver pike.

Still, if you're going to fish for them, you've got to be serious and purposeful about it; you can't go out and deliberately try *not* to catch one; you've got to make the most meticulous and ruthless preparations, then devoutly hope they will all be fruitless.

The choice of bait and equipment is almost equally important as the selection of your companion. Let us start at the bottom, i.e., what you put on the hook. Most people prefer small- or medium-sized chubs from three to five inches long, but I prefer gargantuan chubs—six inches is all right, seven is fine, eight inches is ideal. This is on the announced theory that only the largest pike will swallow them, but actually it is because it is almost impossible to hook a fish through all that amount of bait; ergo, there is all the frivolity of a strike and none of the gruesome aftermath.

The hook should be an ordinary pike hook, which is to say it should be of the size and durability of one you'd use for small hammerhead sharks; nothing smaller or more delicate will suffice.

The leader must be of stout, pliant wire; to use a gut one is like trying to make fast the *Queen Mary* with a clothesline. I prefer a length of wire, red or yellow, that is used with dynamite fuses, because it has a dainty appearance which is quite illusory.

The bobber, which should be placed about four feet above the hook, must be a thing of grace and beauty and a pleasure to behold—if it isn't, then there's no point in fishing on Lower Beaver because the prime reason for being there is to watch the bobber. Nowadays they make all manner of plastic bobbers and Plexiglas bobbers, and no doubt they make throwaway bobbers that come in disposable containers, but these plainly will not do; you've got to have a lovely bobber that floats on the water as trim and perky as a May fly. My favorite—in fact the only one I've used for forty years—is an egg-shaped cork, one half painted yellow, the other green, with a slender pick protruding at each end, which has survived the years and the uncountable pike that have lunged at it with mistaken but vicious intent. It is scarred and faded but still performs with pride—cocked out there on the still water, it is sensitive to whatever skulduggery is going on in the noxious depths beneath.

Nothing much need be said of the line except that it should be stout, or of the rod or pole except that a slightly resilient one is preferable to something you might pick up in the tool shed, such as a rake handle, simply because you can throw out the bait and bobber more easily, and not for any sporting consideration, because there isn't any.

So much for the equipment that is requisite to the actual capture of the pike, except for the instrument that transfers it from the water to the boat. Some unimaginative people use a net and invariably discover the appalling consequences; the pike's teeth, which are like multipointed razor blades, reduce the mesh to tatters, and in the hazardous despicable task of disengaging one from the other, the whole boat becomes slimy and malodorous, thus disrupting the placidity of the outing. So I prefer an old old device that must have been especially designed to cope with either pike or cobras; it has fanged iron wings which you spread apart as you would the jaws of a bear trap, and which spring together when you ram it down on your adversary. It has an efficient and immobolizing influence so that if you absolutely have to bring a pike into the boat, against your every inclination, it is an operation that is quickly over and best forgotten.

As to the means of water transport, it cannot be a canoe or an Adirondack guide boat or any kind of a lightly constructed round-bottomed boat; all of these are too unstable and fickle. And no kind of metal or fiber glass boat is suitable in any way; they are stolidly vulgar in appearance and thunderously noisome. So a flat-bottomed square-ended cedar scow—the kind that Winslow Homer favored—is the perfect vehicle; it is far faster and more responsive than its squat appearance would indicate; it is reliable and pond-worthy; and, most important, it has commodious appointments for bobber fishing, such as a fish box where you can keep the pike out of sight and mind, and not have them slopping all over the boat, and it has seats so arranged that you can recline on one and put up your feet on another. It is an old-shoe kind of boat that has been through every travail and suffered many indignities without taking offense—you feel comfortable and at ease, and slightly proud to be in it.

In hot summer weather, the Lower Beaver pike congregate in six small areas of the pond, all of which have various features in common; they are adjacent to mucky shallows where the pike forage on smaller fish, mostly their own young; in slightly deeper water there are beds of yellow water lilies; and immediately beyond them the pond shelves off steeply into deep water. It is in these cooler depths, just outside the lily beds, that the pike spend their leisure time, and it is there that a bobber fisherman can have some expectancy of successfully coming to grips with one.

Of these locations I am most partial to a place called "the pike beds"; it is on the western shore where a sphagnum bog juts out and from which you have a view across the pond to the low-lying swamp country, with Beaver Mountain in the distance. If the pike aren't being annoyingly rapacious, you can waste a lot of time there in useless meditation.

You row the scow to the pike beds slowly and with gentle stealth, not because there is any fear of alarming the pike (nothing less than a small depth charge will seriously disconcert one), but because haste and noise in bobber-fishing are as unseemly as a toad in a punch bowl—it just is. Furthermore, part of the mystique of all this is that you've got to feel and believe that it requires the most cunning machinations to outwit a pike, which of course isn't the case at all. (It must be understood that the success of the expedition is frought with, and dependent upon, self-deception and hallucination.)

So you steal up to the pike beds with a smug feeling that you've successfully infiltrated enemy territory, and commence your clandestine activities. You position the scow directly over his base of operations, i.e., fifteen yards out from the lily bed, then your companion slips down the anchor (a twenty-five-pound block of concrete will suffice) and snubs the rope, all this causing only the slightest turmoil on the water surface. He then transfers the chubs from the suffocating atmosphere of the bait bucket to a wire mesh container which he lowers into the water and ties to the boat; this not only keeps the chubs lively and happy, which is a most important consideration not only from their point of view, but also because it makes them more attractive to the pike; also a happy chub with a yen for exploration keeps the bobber in a state of exciting titillation. And furthermore, a bait bucket full of morose listless chubs, some of them belly up, can cast a doleful shadow on the proceedings.

While your companion is accommodating the chubs to their satisfaction, you take precautions to ensure against needless aggravations; you put the tackle box in a place where it is least likely to snag your line in a moment of crisis; you put your jug or flask and other emergency equipment where they are instantly at hand; you ship the oars and stow them—then finally you are fully mobilized to do battle with the heathen.

You impale a chub on your hook, strip yards of line off your reel, and cast the whole shebang—chub, bobber, and all—toward but not *into* the lily pads. Trying to catch a pike which is already in a bed of lilies is akin to General Braddock's experience at the Battle of Vincennes. The pike, ensconced in his private forest of tough lily stems, and with no conception of civilized warfare (which is waged in the open, standing in ranks, and preferably to the accompaniment of bagpipes), is a dastardly and unsatisfactory foe. So you have to engage him outside the lily bed and hope that he won't retreat into it once the battle has been joined.

So you toss out your heinous offering ("heinous" is defined as "hateful, odious, abominable; totally reprehensible"), it lands with a splash, the commotion subsides, the bobber begins to twitter as the chub sets forth on an innocent tour of exploration, and you sit there as if you'd just fused a time bomb and were skeptical of your own safety.

What happens after that is conjectural and never the same; you might be sitting there, still tense and awed by the possible consequences of your commitment, still unbelieving that you actually had the temerity to do it, when suddenly, with a slight glupping sound, the bobber pops beneath the surface and is gone into the murky depths, then your loose line streams out as though it were attached to a meteor. This indicates that a pike—a particularly ugly Mafia type of pike—has assaulted your chub, successfully kidnaped it, and is presently speeding it to a private hideout where it can be disposed of at leisure.

Or it might be that there is no immediate encounter—the bobber dips lightly about the still surface, going hither and yon like the Merry Little Breezes, and you have time to settle yourself and arrange your comforts, and feel almost at ease, when, oh my, the bobber takes a dip that is more authoritative than the chub can induce, then there are a series of dips, coming faster, and then the bobber is dancing off with just its stem above water, like a periscope. This means that a satisfied, well-fed pike is scourging your chub, not from any pang of hunger, but because it suits his sadistic whim.

Or you can recline there for an hour or more and become lulled into a state approaching nirvana ("a place or state characterized by freedom from or oblivion to pain, worry and the external world"), and then with no warning your companion emits a grunt, denoting mild interest, and he's looking in the direction of your bobber—and it's not there, it has vanished without trace, then you feel the line streaking out and finally spot the bobber, just beneath the surface, torpedoing away.

The conclusion to any of these happenings is again wholly unpredictable because the initiative, after the pike has seized your chub, is with *him;* you can't instantly snag him and then force him to fight on terrain of your own choice, you have to be exasperatingly patient and let him take the bait wherever he chooses, be it into the lily bed or out into deep water, and when he reaches the place he wants to be, and stops, you have to give him the uninterrupted leisure to swallow it, or to toy with it or to otherwise do what he pleases, and only when you hope that he has it firmly in his mouth do you bring in the slack line until you feel his weight out there on the end, then finally the moment of truth has come—and you give him a mighty strike.

The result will probably be humiliating; you either strike too soon, pulling the mangled chub from his mouth, or you outwit yourself and wait too long, allowing the pike to swallow the bait, disgorge the hook, and escape with infuriating impunity. But sometimes—just sometimes—your strike meets solid resistance, then there is a tense moment of nothing-at-all, during which the dull-witted fish is coming to the realization that he has been foully duped, then he erupts with fury.

If you hooked him in the lily bed, your chances of *not* getting him are excellent; he will slash about in circles, entwining the line about more and more lily stems until it would take a small winch and cable to crank him out of there, so that almost inevitably something will break, or he will tear loose, and you will be free of him. If he rushes the chub to deep water and you hook him *there,* your chances of not boating him aren't nearly as great, but you shouldn't despair; there are logs and weed patches on the bottom around and under which he can snag your line, and there is always the anchor rope—perhaps the only redeeming characteristic of most pike is their God-given gift of wrapping lines around anchor ropes. And finally as a last recourse, there is your companion, who is handling the gaff; if he is the proper sort, he can fumble and bumble with it, and miss countless opportunities to immobolize the fish, and he can contrive other means to bring about a successful nonconclusion for all concerned.

But if all this is unavailing—if finally there is a pike, snapping and snarling and unrepentant, in the scow—then there is nothing for it but to whack him and whack him and whack him behind the ears with a stout cudgel or a length of lead pipe, then clap him into the fish box. Then you can compose your feelings, rearrange the boat, and launch the next foray.

You can continue this feckless campaign of attrition as long as you and/or your companion are incognizant of its asininity; or until all the pike, sated with hate, retire to the lily bed to sulk; or until your bottom becomes paralyzed; or until you have exhausted the bait supply and/or the emergency rations—whatever the reason, you heave up the anchor and go home to late dinner, feeling foolish to be sure, but also feeling that it's all right—in fact better than all right—to pleasure yourself in this fashion if you don't do it more than once a year, on a Sunday.

Fall

1.

A few years ago, on a hot dry late-August afternoon, I was witness to a scene that I had never before encountered—a massive condensed migration of songbirds. I was returning from town to Baker's Clearing, coming down into the river valley, when I noticed them, and stopped the pickup. Only slowly did I realize the enormity of what I was seeing—there were hundreds of thousands, perhaps millions, of birds around and above. They were flying high overhead, and flitting through the tree-tops, and invading the young growth, they were hopping about in the dusty road, and rustling in the dry leaves. It was a tumultuous river of birds—a chittering, chirping, restless spate, funneling south down the valley. There were tanagers and fly-catchers and myriad warblers; there were robins (always an incongruous sight in the deep woods), and thrushes and finches and thrashers and sparrows—all so various and fleeting that I was bug-eyed. And escorting this frenetic exodus, were the nonmigrant winter birds—chickadees, nuthatches, kinglets and woodpeckers. Like Vermonters seeing their guests off on a train, they were calm and normal-seeming amid the bustle and frenzy of the southbound tourists.

I don't know how long it went on—half an hour perhaps—then the channel of birds tapered off as if the floodgate had been closed, and the sound of their passing became remote in the valley below, then the last bird—a fox sparrow—came driving through the woods like a late commuter, and then there was almost silence. But not quite; somewhere a long way off, a pileated woodpecker was probing a dead tree with absorbed and deliberate purpose.

I sensed then what I knew for certain that night when a wicked front, with cold rain and high winds whipped down from Canada; summer was over and fall had come to the Adirondacks.

In a human sense, Adirondack autumn comes on Labor Day. You can feel the end of summer about two o'clock on that afternoon when the main highways begin to clog with southbound traffic. By late afternoon, the cars are crawling bumper to bumper, mile after mile; by midnight the great resorts—Lake George, Saranac, Lake Placid, Speculator, Old Forge—that this morning were teeming centers of fun and frolic are now like forsaken cruise ships with only a skeleton crew on board.

I will confess to feeling wistful about this mass departure, but also slightly smug and superior—like a soldier chosen to defend the ramparts so that the main army can beat an orderly retreat.

Perhaps autumn everywhere—at least in the country—is the contemplative time of year, the adult time. At Baker's Clearing, it most certainly is. The passing of Labor Day brings a glorious quiet to the clearing; there is no clatter of fast little feet on the porches; the dock on Mink Pond is deserted and only the abandoned swimming suits, water wings, and frogman feet are there to remind you that here yesterday was happy Bedlam; there is no yapping of small city dogs, only the two or three Resident Business Dogs are left to go on their important inspection tours in peace and quiet; the boats and canoes lap in their slips, waiting to be put up on the rafters.

A Resident Business Dog relaxes after a frenetic summer.

Now is the time to get down to fundamentals—such as putting the bird feeder in operation, and going to Middle Beaver Pond to see if there will be a cranberry crop this year, and to get some branches off a soft maple in Mink Inlet that has turned a deep red.

It is also the time to pay a few bills and balance your checkbook, but you let that go till next day.

The reaction of the animals in and about Baker's Clearing to this Labor Day transformation is something more than curious; they seem to believe that they have owned the place forever, were temporarily dispossessed, and were merely biding their time to infiltrate back and re-establish their prerogatives. Hardly has the last car left the clearing, and the hush begun, when a couple of deer that you haven't seen before (there are always a dozen or more semitame ones about the clearing, that you get to know intimately) emerge from the swamp and make tentative exploration of the apple trees; coons that have been ravaging the garbage cans and making an infuriating clatter only at night, now climb the porch chairs and glare at you through the window with an evil-innocent, deadpan intensity; and the wood mice—those devils that up to now have been quite happy to live where they belong, i.e., in the woods—now begin a stealthy invasion of the house—down the chimney,

through the woodshed, even up the drainpipe—to re-establish possession and take up winter quarters in their favored abode; and the coyotes that have been secretive while raising their young, come into the clearing and make the night a weird, wondrous, shivering thing.

Autumn on the clearing is the realization of death, which is only a quickened sense of life. The feeling of quiet hurry, of transition, of an erratic but nonetheless fated drift toward winter, is pervasive—sundown each day comes earlier; each morning the green of Beaver Mountain has given further way to the seeping invasion of deadly color, each day when the deer come to the apple trees, the steel blue hair of their winter coats is more pronounced; the black cat, which all summer has shunned humanity, comes with increasing regularity to the kitchen; each day there is a larger build-up of ducks on the marshes.

In the fall it is impossible for me to do any sustained writing; perhaps (and this may sound ridiculous) it is because I feel too well to buckle down. I can't divorce myself from the muted activity, so that there is always something more important to look at or to think about or to feel than whatever it is I am working on. These distractions sometimes take an extreme form, such as the day that the spikehorn buck we called Stupid (he lived constantly on the clearing and became almost a bore) appeared under my apple tree, per usual, then suddenly and crazily, he started to rub his horns against the trunk until the velvet was hanging in bloody tatters around his face.

And the bright windy October day that the clearing was invaded by a great flight of hawks—sparrow hawks, sharp-shins, redtails, broadwings, Coopers, and red-shouldered hawks; they went wheeling and beating about, then in a few hours they were gone.

And then there was that noon on a breezy, hazy day in late September when this thing came fluttering and tumbling

through the air; I thought at first it was just another leaf, then I knew it was a monarch butterfly on its way to the tropics. I saw it for only a little time—a minute perhaps—but there was something innocent and gallant about that weightless thing; it was being buffeted and driven by the wind, but it was on the course it wanted to go, traveling with serenity and purpose,

with no qualms about reaching its destination. It went out of sight over the apple tree, then I got the glasses and picked it up again, kiting along across the pasture. Then it wafted up over the beechwoods and was gone. Good God.

A man can't work with things like that going on.

As fall progresses, the activity becomes more purposeful and energetic; the beavers get established in their winter quarters and start collecting underwater food beds; the loons make longer and more frequent training flights in preparation for the final trip; the brook trout move into running water to spawn; the red squirrels that seemingly have been scarce all summer materialize in hoards and go to work on the cone crop; and the otters that heretofore have stayed fairly close to home go off on extended circuits through the ponds and streams and river.

On the Baker Tract human activity gears itself in similar fashion; now is the time to put up storm windows, make sure your water system won't freeze, and otherwise snug down for the winter; now, when the sap is out of the trees and the ground is dry, is the time to start cutting hardwood logs and to rough out the winter haul roads, and to shoe the horses with ice calks; the time to go bullhead fishing at night, with a bottle of antifreeze; to stop whatever you're doing at the first faraway sound of geese. It is the time, also, to be alert for outlaws jacking deer at night, and to stock the hunting camp on Split-rock Pond with provisions; and to time your visit to town, for supplies and mail, so you can go to the Mountain View bar to see on television the last innings of a world series game. (Once I arrived just in time to see Mr. Mazeroski of the Pittsburgh Pirates hit a series-winning home run and go waltzing around the bases in ecstatic glee.) It is time also to make gentle fun of those tourists who are known locally as "the leaf people"—elderly ladies mostly, but sometimes escorted by a gentleman in knicker-bockers and tweed cap—who are making a pilgrimage to see the autumn foliage. They are delightful and unobtrusive, they have sedate picnics and clean up their trash, and we are happy and proud that their opinion coincides exactly with ours, i.e., that our vicinity in autumn is indeed the very most entrancing place in the world, without, as Mister Toad's judge said, "Any benefit of the doubt, because there isn't any."

On these autumn trips to the settlements, the foliage is an invariable subject of learned discussion—what sort of weather, for instance, makes for the best color, wet or dry? Hot or cold? When will the color reach its peak? That sort of thing. I personally believe that I am authoritative (so does everyone else); each year the color is brilliant and beautiful beyond memory or belief, and each year the high tide comes in the first week of October. After that, the garrish reds and oranges of the maples begin to fade, and their leaves to fall, and then is the loveliest time of all—on a clear Indian-summer afternoon, the hardwood forests are a swan song of sun and shadow, of soft yellow and pale poplar green, and the falling leaves come sifting down through the branches. This is the nostalgic time to be in the woods, the time to be quiet and have no particular business in mind. It is the time to sense, but not bemoan the fact, that you're getting older.

The fall color lasts long enough so that you become glutted with its demanding beauty—then there comes a day, usually about the twentieth of October, when an arctic front arrives, bringing with it gale winds and driving rain that sweep across the ridges, and the leaves come storming off the trees in swirling clouds, and the beechnuts patter down like hail, and the next day, when the front has passed and there is a frosty stillness, it is a relief to discover that the woods are steel gray and bare, stripped down to their clean essentials. The time of nostalgia is gone and there is a fresh excitement abroad.

Now is the beechnut season and, if there is a good or lush supply of nuts, all the birds and animals that aren't strictly carnivorous forsake other food to feast on them—bears get as fat as only bears can get; deer, coons, partridges, bluejays, squirrels, even foxes stuff on them. And the chipmunks!—the good lord save a deer hunter from the mobs of chipmunks that infest the beech woods on a clear dry November afternoon—the buck chipmunks sit, each on his homestead stump, and keep up a dissonant chirping chorus, and when they tire of this practice they crash around in the dry leaves, chasing each other and engaging in mortal combat; and all the while this is going on, their ladies scurry about, like hags at a bargain counter, in an insatiable search for nuts. If you are a hunter, waiting for the first intimation of a deer, you can learn to hate chipmunks, quite fast, and with no prior instruction.

The first snowstorm.

I wait for the first snow with huge impatience; it comes at night after a time of high wind and growing cold, then the next morning there is a white blanket of silence, a hush, a breathless expectancy—it is a time to move slowly and speak in whispers.

For me, animal tracks in fresh snow evoke, as nothing else, the natural mysteries—why did this pair of otters forsake Lonesome Pond, where they could have a year-long glut of frogs and polliwogs and crayfish, and go three miles overland to Wolf Creek? What was this mink doing on the clearing, two miles from water? And the fisher that was beelining for Beaver Mountain, then abruptly changed its course and went down Mink Inlet—what was on *its* mind? This fox—why did it carry a chipmunk in its mouth for half a mile, then sit down and decide to eat it? The bobcat track that laces everywhere from Lonesome Pond to high on Peaked Mountain—was the animal on an aimless prowl or did it have some purpose in mind? And where was it now? And what doing? And why? And where would it be tomorrow? Animal tracks in snow are easy to follow and usually lead to no conclusion, so they evoke the perturbing mysteries that man will never clue; the animals are superior in their innocence and aloof from his ken.

Crossbills and siskins.

2.

After that first November snowstorm there may be some warm spells and periods of sickly east winds when the dripping woods are silent and shrouded, and every breathing thing waits in morose quiet, but the portents of winter are daily more in evidence—the rutting of the bucks comes to a climax of insane lust, then tapers off; the younger bears and the chipmunks go into hibernation; Mink Pond freezes over and the last of the ducks move out; the siskins and pine grosbeaks and crossbills arrive from northern Canada; all but the hardiest of hunters break camp and come out of the woods. And then there comes a time, each year about the twentieth of November, that the wind comes from the north, and a cloud bank settles in, ominous and massive and dark, and the thermometer goes down, always down, and then finally, like an invasion that has been long planned and thoroughly organized, the snow sweeps down.

Almost surely on Thanksgiving Day, when we assemble to toast our blessings and sate our bellies, we will arrive on snowshoes and have it in mind that the easy times are over and that winter is at hand.

Before Labor Day, the water in Frank Pond begins to cool and the brook trout come from the depths where they have been since early July and move into more shallow water, and once again become vulnerable to fly fishermen. At the same time, the urge to reproduce stirs in them and they become increasingly restless.

Frank Pond is shaped like a crookneck summer squash, with the outlet at the narrow end. Its watershed is covered almost entirely with hardwood timber so there is no amber discoloration to the water from softwoods, as there is in most Adirondack ponds. Also, there is no real inlet—just two little wet-weather brooks—and the pond is almost entirely spring-fed. This combination of circumstances makes for truly gin-clear water; when the light is right, you can see the bottom at a depth of twenty-five feet or more, and if you look carefully and have good eyes, you can see, almost as deep down, the flicking white fins of the trout.

Midway down the pond, at the sharp crook, a shelving granite ledge juts out and into the water, and there is a sort of cave which is a fine place for scuba divers to explore, and where trout like to be at certain seasons.

If you sit on the ledge in May or June or early in July, you will probably see many trout. They won't be going anyplace

Frank Pond from the ledge.

in particular; they will be moving about erratically, looking for food, or perhaps not moving much at all, just taking their comfort and passing the time. You are likely to see trout of all sizes consorting with one another.

In August, you won't see any trout at all from the ledge; they are out in deeper water.

In late August or early September they will reappear about the ledge, but almost surely they won't be behaving as they did in June—they will be going somewhere with a purpose. You'll be watching the depths and seeing nothing alive down there except newts (Frank Pond has more newts than any pond I know), and then a school of trout will come by, following the shore line and about eight feet down. They are like sight-seers on a guided tour—not hurrying, but moving along with determination, and not stopping or going on diversionary side trips. They pass out of sight and then presently another group —five, ten, maybe as many as twenty fish—will coast into sight, pass in review, and disappear in the same direction as the other had gone. And then sooner or later other schools will come by. Each school will be composed of fish of almost identical size—two-pounders in one, fifteen-inchers in another, and so on—and despite the fact that no two groups ever seem to intermingle or have any communication, they will all be going, at any particular time, in the same direction. One day, they will all be going clockwise around the shore line; the next day they may all be on a counterclockwise course. I have no explanation for this.

I am sure that on these apparently purposeful excursions about the pond the fish are looking for suitable circumstances, preferably running water, in which to spawn. A brook trout's instinct is to go up the inlet of a pond to do this, but Frank has no inlet, so, unless they spawn on the deep spring holes (we have no way of knowing whether some of them do this), they are

Spawning.

obliged to go to the extreme narrow end, just above the outlet, where there is a sufficient movement of water to satisfy them.

As a consequence, about the middle of September, the trout begin to move from the main body of the pond into the narrows, and they congregate there in water about four feet deep, and about one hundred yards above the shallow extreme narrows where they will eventually spawn. They are still in schools of like-sized fish, but of necessity the schools are close together, so that a fish butcher, using almost any sort of lure, could fill a bushel basket of the ravenous things in short order and with small exertion. At this time it is easy to tell the males from the females—the former have deep-red sides and bellies; the females aren't nearly as brilliant.

For about two weeks there is a build-up of fish in the upper narrows, then one day about October 1, a few will have moved down to the spawning grounds, selected spots to their particular liking, and will be preparing redds; you can see them fanning the silt away with their tails to expose the clean sand beneath. While they are doing this, there is an almost constant infiltration of fish from the upper narrows; they come down in twos and threes, and sometimes in larger parties, and there is no longer any size distinction among them—big and small come down together. They come down fast, darting along, as though they were chary of being in such shallow water; they explore as far down as they can go, poke about briefly, then scoot back to the safety of the deeper water.

Within a week, the spawning is well under way, and there will be at least three hundred trout on the grounds—a water area about one hundred yards long and ten wide, with a depth of from one to two feet—engaged in various activities. Some fish are actually spawning, the females suddenly and sporadically slithering on their sides against the bottom as they eject the eggs, the males in close attendance except when they dart off to combat intruders. Some fish are still preparing redds. The great majority of trout, however, are interloping marauders; they cruise about like bandits and do their best to be a disrupting influence. Whatever they are doing, all the trout have lost caution; you couldn't scare them off the grounds, for long, if you tried. It would seem that they would be easy prey for any mink, otter, bear, or owl that chanced that way, but I have seen no instance of any of these predators making use of the bounty.

The spawning lasts about five weeks; the first fish to make redds complete their business and move back into deeper water, other fish usurp the same redds, and are followed by others, and they by still others until, in early November, there are only a few late starters in the narrows. Then they too are gone, and you wouldn't know there was a fish in the pond.

Keeping watch on this spawning routine is hugely satisfying to us for a particular reason—the trout wouldn't be spawning in the narrows, in fact they wouldn't be in Frank Pond at all, if we hadn't brought it about.

Trout were a staple of diet, along with venison, in Squire Baker's household, but there is no record of any being caught in Frank Pond; there must have been a few, but apparently not enough to arouse interest.

There is an occasional record of a trout being caught there in the 1890s and early 1900s; after that there is none. It seems that the perch, sunfish, and golden shiners which infested the pond had finally made life impossible for them.

For years we entertained the notion of "reclaiming" the pond, which is to say that we wanted to eradicate the trash fish and restock it with trout, but the cost of rotenoning the pond, which was the only feasible tactic then available, was prohibitive. So all we did was talk about what a good idea it was.

Then in 1958 we learned of a new chemical—Toxopherine—that had been used on an experimental basis in many of the states and some of the Canadian provinces, always with spectacularly efficient results and with apparently no serious consequences. It was inexpensive to buy and easy to apply; the only drawback seemed to be that the water where it was used was apt to remain toxic for a longer period than would be the case with rotenone. We concluded to try it.

First we built a barrier dam on the outlet, just below the pond, to prevent any undesirable fish from getting back to it, then in October we applied the poison.

The first dying fish surfaced four hours later. The next day the holocaust was awesome and grim—dead and dying fish were littered everywhere—and within two days the decimation was total. A week later the dead fish had rotted away and vanished without trace, and the pond looked pristine as ever. The job had been done and now all we had to do was stock the trout.

When the ice went out the following May, we put a dozen caged trout in about fifteen feet of water. They were dead the next morning. In August, we tried again—with the same result. That fall, we tried a stocking of five hundred six- to seven-inch trout. In the spring there wasn't a sign of them. Another planting in the fall of 1960 was proved the following spring to have been a failure.

By this time—two and a half years after the irreparable step —we were having the most sober thoughts on what we had done, and were feeling anything but smug about our arbitrary tinkering. We surmised, hopefully, that there was so little water coming into the pond, and going out of it, that the poison wasn't flushing out of the deep pockets on the bottom.

In the autumn of 1961, we stocked again.

I remember well going over there with a friend on May 13 of the following spring. It was a quiet afternoon, and a vast hatch of small duns was coming off the water, and the pond surface was a turmoil of rising trout. We damn near cried.

Since then, the trout have prospered beyond expectation or wildest hope. At first we were doubtful that there would be enough natural food for them, since we had destroyed all the small fish on which they feed, but there was nothing to worry about on that account; from May to mid-October the insect life in the pond is so prolific and various that the trout can't begin to make full use of it. It isn't happenstance that fishing with dry flies is unproductive more often than not; the trout are sating themselves on the nymphs before they get to the surface, shed their casings, and become flies. In addition to this superabundant insect life, there is a lush supply of plankton in the water which is available the year round to the trout; in winter time they lie down there under the ice and suck it in through their gills and wax big. Unlike trout in most Adirondack ponds, the Frank Pond trout grow steadily and fast throughout the year;

a six-incher in the fall will be at least eleven inches the following spring, sixteen inches the following year, and about twenty
the one after that. The largest taken so far was a four-year-old
male; it was twenty-two inches long and weighed four pounds,
four ounces.

We wanted a natural self-sufficient trout pond, not one that
depended on the artificiality of constant restocking, but natural
reproduction of fish in the pond was a problem from the start,
due to the lack of a proper inlet. The trout spawned in the
outlet narrows all right, but nothing came of it because the
bottom there, beneath the silt which the fish fan away, is fine
sand and not the coarse pebble-sized gravel which is requisite
for good spawning grounds. (Eggs lying on sand are gobbled
up by the trout themselves, or are washed away, but when they
are laid on coarse gravel, they sink into the crevices and some
of them—a minute percentage—are safe.)

The spawning grounds.

For three years after the first successful stocking, there was no evidence of reproduction. In the fall of 1965, during the height of the spawning, we put a small quantity of coarse gravel in the extreme narrows of the pond. Perhaps we didn't put in enough, perhaps we were too late in doing it; anyhow, there were no visible results the following spring.

That summer we carried in a great deal more gravel.

The following May, I paddled about the pond shore and made a discovery almost as exciting as that day, five years be-

Spring—two-pounders.

fore, when the trout were thrashing after the duns; in the shallows, lurking close to the leather-leaf bushes that overhang the shore, were hundreds of tiny fry.

In retrospect, the Frank Pond experiment seems to have been an unqualified success; we re-established the trout, and today the pond is a thriving habitat, not only for them, but for beavers, otters, and muskrats; for newts and frogs; for an infinite variety of insect life; and for all native birds which live on or close to the water. The only things notable for their happy absence are the small coarse fish, so that presently, and from our point of view, the situation there is perfect, and apparently in balance, and apparently natural.

But is it? Is that poison we put in there totally dissipated and totally and forever without influence in the waters that it permeated? We don't know—we simply don't know, but I would guess this—no one associated with the Frank Pond ordeal would favor another such experiment. We played at being God and seem to have got away with it, but once is enough.

3.

If you have an interest in trapping beaver, October is the time to get about your territory to find, exactly, where they are located. This is not only because it is a fine invigorating time to travel the woods, but for two practical reasons—the beaver are almost certainly situated in the houses and dens where they plan to winter, and furthermore they make an ostentatious display of their intentions by amassing "food beds" of fresh-cut hardwood limbs from trees that they have felled. These beds are immediately adjacent to their proposed homes, underwater of course, so that in winter the animals can get to them without exposing themselves to the bitter air. After the ice and snow have come, you can walk right over these food beds and never suspect they are there or that there are any beaver in the vicinity. Conversely, if you make too early a survey—say in August—you can get an erroneous conception of where you're going to find them in the winter, because some animals, like affluent retired folk, have two homes, one for summer and another for winter. Also, two-year-old beaver form attachments, move away from home, and set up quarters of their own. Almost always they do this in autumn, so I say again—mid-October is the time to find out where they will be when trapping time comes in March.

Not all beaver are transients; they don't abandon their homes unless there is a reason, in fact a necessity, for it, caused by overcrowding or a food shortage, or both, or due to their summer

Beaver house at the High Dam and the proprietor. The house is in deep water and occupied the year round.

house becoming untenable in winter when the water freezes to the bottom so that they can't have access to the food bed. In such cases, the summer home is usually on the north-facing shore of the pond and the winter one on the south-facing shore.

But not always. For three years now an interesting situation has been transpiring on Splitrock Pond. This pond has been, within my memory, the most favored beaver site on the tract. Whereas all the other ponds have been forsaken by them at one time or another, then repossessed, there have been continuously active colonies on Splitrock, sometimes as many as five houses, for at least forty-five years. This is because the pond is surrounded by hardwoods, not conifers, so that there is an abundant and sustaining supply of choice beaver food—yellow and white birch, soft and hard and striped maple, witchhopple, and, even after all these years of beaver predation, some of their favored poplar.

At any rate, in September of 1964, a new house came into being in the corner of the north-facing bay and from the strenuous activity going on—a large well-mudded house with an affluent food bed in front—it was apparent that some earnest beaver intended to winter there. When Ed Maunton, who is knowledgeable about these animals, saw it, he said the situation was impossible—they'd be frozen out, he said, because the house entrance was barely a foot under water, and the food bed was in scarcely deeper water. He said the beaver would be gone by February.

He was right. When trapping season came, the beaver had moved to an old house on the south-facing shore, a mile away, and were living in reduced circumstances, with bad insulation and no food bed. Nor did they repossess their former house when spring came; it remained abandoned all that summer and the following winter, and then in September another pair of beaver, or possibly the same ones, took over the premises, mudded it up, compiled a flamboyant food bed, and endured the same sad fiasco.

This situation isn't too surprising because beaver don't have the sagacity, the know-how, or even the intuition that many people ascribe to them—except in dam building. Much has been written, for instance, about how they can fell a tree exactly where they want it to lie. Well, in my experience this is total nonsense; I know something about logging and how to cut a tree in such a way that it will come down where you want it, and I have examined thousands of trees that beaver have cut, and I have yet to find a tree that didn't fall the way it naturally leaned. On pond shores, beavers have great success in falling their trees into the water—which is precisely where they want to have them, but this is solely because trees lean toward the light, and so of course will fall that way. But beaver, working on a small, densely wooded stream, will hang up a dozen trees for every one they succeed in getting to the ground where they can make use of it, either for food or for dam building.

A visit to such a place makes you feel sorry for the frustrated animals; everywhere are cut trees, dead or dying, lodged in other trees of varieties that beaver don't like to eat or that are too big for them to cope with; always there are a dam and pond which get increasingly higher and bigger, drowning whatever timber the beaver haven't already killed. The reason for this is that beaver hate to go overland any farther than they absolutely have to travel, so they keep raising the dam level to give them easy access to more and more timber—creating a waste and desolation that at first sight are awesome and morbid.

Except for the dead trees, there is nothing morbid about a beaver pond—it teems with activity. Mink and otter thrive on the aquatic life; deer swarm about the mucky shores; ducks, especially the wood ducks, blacks, hooded mergansers, and other puddlers, are attracted by the nesting situations; bears come to wallow; hawks, particularly the broadwings, and great-horned owls are fascinated by the food supply and the dead trees on which to perch; tree swallows and all other birds that like watery, semistagnant places find it glorious; even trout can usually flourish, so a beaver pond is anything but morbid.

Inevitably, beaver exhaust the food supply in such a pond, and move away to greener woods, then the dam deteriorates, and the water recedes, and bear grass grows up on the exposed muck, and the timber rots away, and there comes into being what is known as "an old beaver flow," which is one of the more distinctive features of Adirondack geography. Finally the forest grows back and the beaver return.

There are many such places, in various stages of transformation, on the Baker Tract. Presently, the most prosperous is on a small stream, west of Frank Pond, that runs through flat, low-lying country. The area was cut for balsam pulp twenty years ago (the heavy stand of pine was not cut), and two years later a small colony of beaver became established and managed to survive, but they didn't reproduce in any quantity. Then ten years ago the pine was clean-cut, leaving great open areas along the stream, creating ideal conditions for the reproduction of poplar—the most favored of all beaver food. In 1964, the poplar grew above the raspberry briars and began to burgeon, and the beaver immediately proliferated. Today there are five contiguous dams on the stream and at least three colonies of beaver established in a veritable beaver Eden, with no prospect that they will eat away the bounty for some time to come.

The most prosperous beaver establishment on the tract.

The most interesting beaver situation is at the High Dam, located on a small stream that drains the southeastern watershed of Beaver Mountain and is one of the inlets to Mink Pond. When I was a boy, the beaver had been there long before, and moved away, and the place was a defunct beaver flow. Thirty-five years later, after we had logged the area, beavers built a new dam in the exact spot where the old one had been. They have been there since then and have created the highest and mightiest dam—it floods the valley for a third of a

The High Dam.

mile—that I have ever seen. It is seventeen feet high and as broad at the base. I couldn't estimate how many tons of wood and stones and mud and leaves and sod, or how many beaver hours, went into its construction, and it is maintained in perfect working order, which is to say that water is always trickling over the top. It is a formidable and magnificent creation and, despite the forest destruction it has caused, we are delighted with it and take a proprietary pride in the beavers.

This talent for dam building must be largely instinctive and not acquired. Some young beaver may get instruction from their parents, but certainly not all, because on Blackwell's Stillwater, for instance, young beaver have no opportunity to learn about dam building because there are no dams. The stillwater, twelve miles long, has for years had numerous beaver colonies and from time to time a young couple, venturing forth on their own, move up one of the feeder streams and matter-of-factly build a practical dam without any supervision.

Incredible as this ability is, it is not miraculous, and I don't think it's thoughtful, and it can be frustrated by human guile; we proved this on Splitrock in 1953, when three colonies of beaver ganged together to build a great dam at the outlet. We didn't mind at first, but when they raised the pond level by three feet and began to drown the trees along the shore line, we dynamited the dam. The beaver rebuilt it; we blew it again. This trial of wits and perseverance went on all summer, then we blew a gap in the dam and installed a sixteen-foot culvert, with the mouth well upstream. The beaver promptly built a dam, constructed as usual in a practical fashion, on top of the culvert, but neglected to plug the mouth. They tried to rectify the situation by putting increasing amounts of stuff around and on top, but the simple problem of plugging the upstream hole was new and incomprehensible, and they never did solve it. They finally abandoned the project.

If we left the beaver strictly alone, there would soon be few, if any, on the tract; they would eat the available food supply and either die out or move away. So we trap the surplus.

The proprietor on a tour of inspection.

The "surplus" is not as arbitrary a thing as it might seem, and it has largely to do with the food circumstances appertaining to each colony. The prosperous beaver on the small stream mentioned above, for instance, are in no present danger of exhausting the poplar, but eventually they would multiply and bring it about, so we try to trap enough to keep the population relatively static; Splitrock Pond has food in sufficient quantity to perpetuate two colonies; Frank Pond can support one at the most; the High Dam, on the other hand, has a shrinking supply due to the beaver drowning far more of it than they use, and the available food is of inferior quality—mostly beech and ash —so we try to leave just enough beaver to keep the dam in working order; on the three Beaver Ponds—Lower, Middle, and Mud all with marshy sphagnum shores—decent food is almost nonexistent, and animals living there are on a bare-subsistence diet—spruce, tamarack, hazel, and alder are about all there is —so whenever a colony moves into one of them, we try to eradicate it.

A bit of beaver sculpture at the High Dam. Apparently two animals of different height worked on the project—the smaller did the neck work and gave up, then the larger took over and finished the job.

Trapper.

The beaver in each particular place tend to vary in size, condition, and procreative ability, due to the quantity and quality of their food; Splitrock and Frank Pond beaver can attain a tremendous size—the largest I ever saw was a female from Splitrock that weighed almost seventy pounds—and they raise large families, as many as six to a litter. The High Dam beavers don't tend to grow as large, although there is presently in residence one venerable gargantuan animal, and I've never seen a trapped female from there with more than four embryos. Those in the Beaver Ponds are apt to be skinny and have three young or less.

Twelve years ago we started a thoughtful, as opposed to a catch-as-catch-can, effort to control the beaver so that we could always have them in reasonable numbers. At that time the tract was swarming with them—we estimated one hundred and fifty, or over—and that winter we trapped sixty-five. The next year we took about forty, and thereafter we've taken between fifteen and twenty, which seems about the right number to keep the population in secure circumstances.

Trapping beaver is work for an expert—of which I am not one—and no one else. The legal season is usually in March and April, when the furs are prime, and that is the hardest time of all to get them because they are usually working under the ice and rarely come out on the banks. This means you have to use "ladder sets." A ladder set is made by chopping a hole through the ice in the proximity of a house, and placing underwater an intricate arrangement of poles which are stuck into the bottom muck, and to which the trap, baited with poplar twigs, is attached.

Sometimes, especially on streams where there is open water, you can use less complicated sets, but it's absolutely essential that you devise them so that the animals drown quickly; if you don't, they will almost surely "wring out" and escape. This is not only heartless and unnecessary; it precludes the probability of catching such animals again, for beaver quickly become wise to the fact that there is a bumbling trapper in the vicinity, and, when aware of this, they sulk in their homes for weeks at a time, or else they become so frightened that they take off for waters unknown.

We leave most of our beaver trapping to Ed Maunton, because he is the most proficient in the business. I have been with him when he has trapped dozens, and the beaver are always dead in the trap, and there are never any wring-outs. Mostly, now, he uses the new Connibear trap, which won the "humane trap" award; they are efficient in many situations and kill instantly, but sometimes he still has to use the conventional steel trap. Sometimes, too, he encounters a particular beaver that requires a good deal of sophisticated chicanery to catch.

There was such an animal on Splitrock in 1963, when we were camped and trapping there. Ed made a routine ladder set with a conventional trap, so placing it that the beaver would hopefully put its left paw on the pan to steady itself while it reached with its right to draw the bait to its teeth, and the next morning the bait was gone and the trap untouched. Maunton, disgruntled as always when something goes amiss, rebaited the trap, and the same fiasco occurred the following night, and the one after that, and the next, with Maunton becoming more and more disgusted and horrified. On the fifth morning, standing there at the hole and surveying the outrageous situation, he suddenly exploded with the equivalent of "Eureka," then explained that this animal he was dealing with was a left-handed beaver, one that pulled food to its mouth with its left paw and not its right. He rearranged the trap and smugly

announced that he'd have the animal tomorrow, caught by its right paw. I'm damned if he didn't.

Over the past twelve years, Ed has averaged about twelve dollars per skin—as much as twenty-four dollars for a blanket pelt and as little as three dollars for an immature one—and he figures that he makes one dollar an hour. He also figures that this is vacation time so it makes a pleasing addition to his income, but it isn't easy to come by; it entails perhaps fifteen miles of snowshoeing each day, a lot of underwater work in frigid weather, and an hour and a half of time to flesh out and stretch the skin of each beaver. The meat is an added bonus.

There is no better meat in the world; it is tender, dark red, without game taste, and nutritious. Those people who have tried to eat it and proclaim it to be inedible didn't know how to prepare it or to cook it, or are innocently prejudiced against the idea of it. It is absolutely necessary to cut off all the oily and bad-tasting external fat; if you do this, and then slice the meat into steaks, and pan-broil it with some beef fat, quickly and rare, it is without compare. The loins and hindquarters are the best, and the age of the beaver makes no difference so long as it is in good condition; an old animal is as fine as, or better than, a young one. In the spring of 1958, Maunton and I ate it twice a day for forty-two days and didn't tire of it.

Beaver on the Baker Tract have no natural enemies except man. Possibly a bear or a bobcat or even a coyote might get a very occasional one, and it is likely that an old buck mink might sometimes kill a young beaver, but I don't know it. Most animals seem to ignore beaver and in turn beaver mind their own business.

The beaver on the tract are secure for the foreseeable future if we continue to control them. The situation poses an interesting historical question: what brought about their near extinction in the nineteenth century? It has been assumed, in fact taken for granted, that the trappers were responsible. I doubt it; the virgin forest, dominated on the pond shores and along the streams and river, by towering stands of conifers, was not a suitable habitat for them, and in the limited areas where they could survive, they brought about their own extinction by exhausting the food supply. That is what would happen on the Baker Tract if we left them alone.

4.

Bears, when they aren't denned for the winter, are great roamers and move about in unpredictable fashion, so the only time you can go looking for one on the tract with any probability of success is in late fall, when there is a lush supply of beechnuts—bears have a gluttonous passion for these and haunt the beech woods—so you can at least narrow down the places where one is likely to be. At other seasons, encountering one is entirely a fortuitous proposition.

In bygone times hunters—including "D. Boon"—used hounds to seek out bears and either bring them to bay or track them to where they were denned, and in either case the actual shooting of them was an easy matter. Or they trapped them, just as easy. Today the use of hounds and traps for such work is illegal in New York, so that hunters and other people interested in a bear confrontation are left to their own devices, which usually prove to be inadequate. (I am talking about bears in the wild, not about "garbage dump" bears that have been seduced and corrupted into loutish clowns that beguile tourists and that are shot in some numbers on the opening day of the hunting season.)

There aren't a great many bears on the tract; every time

A hand-forged bear trap, made about 1880, and
the skull of a medium-sized bear.

one is sighted it is a "happening," and when one is shot it
is a historic event, but there are apparently many more now
than there were in Baker's time.

In the years between 1900 and 1948, there are only three
records of bears being taken. We have a pencil sketch by
Winslow Homer dated 1908, of a small bear being carried on a
pole by two men, and John Byrne told me of killing two cubs
in the winter of 1936; he was fox-hunting with hounds which
inadvertently smelled them out in their den (the hounds were

terrified by their discovery and retreated to John in dismay); he backtracked them to the den and was able to slaughter the dormant inmates. (Why he did this I don't know, because he was an infinitely kind man and had no taste for bear meat; maybe it was his first bear experience and his first opportunity to kill one or two, and he got carried away. Despite various opportunities after that, he never killed another.)

Since that time a dozen or more bears have been killed on the Baker Tract and the territory immediately adjacent to it, and in the summer of 1967 there were at least thirty "sightings," which is not to say that they were thirty different bears, because I had seven of these encounters and am almost certain I saw one particular bear four different times. It was a young lanky, ludicrous, unco-ordinated bear that ran as though its legs were made of rubber so that they flailed out in all directions like a windmill gone berserk.

I think there are presently about ten bears addicted to the general area of the tract. I use that word "addicted" because bears don't seem to have a specific home place, a small area that they inevitably return to, the way deer do. Again unlike deer, their territory is enormous and they wander it erratically, with no apparent precision or purpose; a deer on our tract has a radius of action of perhaps a mile (rutting bucks excepted), and where it is and what it is doing are usually explicable and often predictable, but a bear will roam the whole tract, and beyond, seemingly with no specific intentions. He can be wallowing in the mud at the High Beaver Dam one day, digging out a wasps' nest on Peaked Mountain the next, stuffing on a deer carcass at some faraway place the day after that. An adult bear is usually a solitary wanderer and, being omnivorous, he takes food where he finds it and not necessarily where he knows it to be, and they seem to be opportunists about food, taking what appeals to them and what is at hand, but not specifically seeking out any particular thing. Once they've found something to their liking—a windfall of raspberries or blueberries, or a dead deer, or preferably a number of winter-killed deer—they'll stick with the bounty until it's gone, then prowl on to something else. I think carrion, fresh or otherwise, beguiles a bear more than anything else—with the possible exception of beechnuts. In a

A bear "nest."

good nut year they start climbing the trees in August, when the nuts are "in the milk," and they make what some misguided woodsmen call "nests"—great accumulations of broken branches up in the tops of the beech trees. They aren't nests at all; the bear has simply got up there, as high as he can go, and then swiped in all the branches within his reach to get the nuts off them. (More than anything, I would like to surprise a bear doing this, but I never have.) After the nuts fall to the ground in October, bears snout great troughs in the leaves to find them and make so much noise and are so consumed by greed that they lose their usual alertness. I once walked up on a bear so engrossed that he didn't know I was sitting almost on top of him; he raised his head only occasionally to chomp and slobber like a hog, and never knew I was there.

Bears are reputed by some people to be killers of deer and livestock, and they are generally renowned as depredators of camps and atrocious nuisances. They are all of these things, at certain times and under certain circumstances, but by and large we have amicable relations with them on the tract; they almost never invade our garbage dump, perhaps because we burn it as often as the weather permits, and for some inexplicable reason they have never molested our wild apple trees (the good lord help an apple-laden tree that a bear gets into), and only once has a bear attacked our livestock; this was about twenty-five years ago, when a big one broke into the pigpen, raked our boar across the flank, and chased him into the swamp. The hog escaped somehow and languished in a mud wallow down there for a week, then staggered home and in due course recovered sufficiently to resume his functions.

Every now and then a bear commits a public nuisance which defies explanation; almost yearly, one or more of them prowl the posted lines of the tract and rip down the aluminum signs with their teeth; once a bear invaded the porch of our hunting camp on Splitrock and broke open an old refrigerator, although there was no food, and nothing smelly, in it; one summer another bear cut a swath across the clearing and seemed to have nothing better on his mind than to break down the poles to which the bluebird boxes were attached—the bluebirds had long since nested and gone. Why do they do this sort of mischief? Curiosity? Perversity? A boorish desire to throw their great weight around? An acquired grudge against humans? It could be any of these things or a combination.

I doubt that black bears are consistent killers of any other animal except in specific instances relating to a particular bear. I know this to be true on the Baker Tract; there has been free-roaming livestock, including sheep, for over a hundred years and, except for the lugubrious hog incident, I am not aware of any others. I have examined hundreds of dead deer that weren't shot, but I haven't the slightest evidence that a bear killed any of them.

I know of only two instances where a bear killed anything larger than mice or chipmunks (they can dig these out of their homes); the first was witnessed by a friend of mine and his fishing companion on a remote pond adjacent to the tract. They watched a doe and her fawn dash into the water, pursued by a bear, and swim desperately in circles to escape it, but it was hopeless (bears are fast, strong swimmers), and this one was soon almost on top of the fawn, whereupon the doe turned toward shore, with the fawn and bear following. (It was the men's opinion that the bear could easily have caught the fawn in the water but preferred to let it get ashore.) The three animals dashed into the woods and out of sight and for a short time there was a confused rumpus—high-pitched blatting and much crashing about—then silence. When the men went to investigate, they found two cubs feeding on the fawn; neither the doe nor the mother bear was in sight, nor did they reappear.

The second instance came to my attention on November 23, 1964, while hunting with Ed Maunton in the Mud Beaver swamp. By happenstance, we came on a bear den, recently contrived under the roots of a blown-down tree that was on the side of a deeply shaded knoll (it was dark as a pocket there), and in and around the den was evidence that something fascinating and gruesome had happened—everywhere there were mats of bear hair, enormous bear turds—the largest I've seen— which were comprised mostly of bear hair and undigested bone. Further investigation (we spent most of the day at it) turned up the skinned skull of a small bear (the experts in the Conservation Department later concluded that it was a two-year-old female), and the right thigh, leg, and foot bones. That was all we could find of the remains of one bear that had been eaten by another; there weren't even any pieces of skin, and the only edible matter that remained was the brains inside the skull.

How had all this come about? The evidence of course was wholly circumstantial, but Ed and I pieced it together to our almost perfect satisfaction; the small bear had come that way and taken infinite pains to construct and furnish a den (it was lined with basketfuls of spruce tips and dry ferns that it had collected from an acre around), then it had retired and probably drowsed off; the second bear, which must have been a monster in every sense of the word, sniffed it out, killed it, and thereafter remained on or about the premises for about a week, alternately stuffing and sleeping, until it had consumed the entire carcass.

Skeptics will have some pertinent doubts about our analysis

of all this, but Ed and I think we have valid answers. How do we know the big bear actually killed the smaller one, that the smaller one wasn't already dead when the big one found it? Answer—a sick or a wounded bear, about to die, wouldn't have made that snug den for itself; no animal would behave that way. And how do we know it wasn't the big bear that was asleep in the den and was infuriated by the intrusion of the smaller one? Well, for one thing, when a bear finally dens and goes to sleep, it has long since stopped eating, so that its stomach has shrunk to a small nonfunctioning thing about the size of a coconut; it seems unlikely that it could suddenly be awoken, make a kill, and start to gorge again. Also, young bears and perhaps especially young females are apt to den much earlier than the old males. It may be that bears become more and more carnivorous as they get older and stay abroad longer after snow has covered the herbivorous food. All you have to do to prove this on the Baker Tract is to tour around in December and January and examine the tracks of any bear that is still about; you won't find any small or even medium-sized tracks. (There is one pathetic and occasional exception to this; you may find the tracks of one, or a pair, of bereft motherless cubs who don't know enough to den up. A few years ago one of our hunters killed a female bear that had a cub in tow, and all the following winter through mid-February I saw its tracks in that near vicinity, then I never saw them again. There is a supposition that a mother bear dens her young and snugs them in, then goes elsewhere to winter by herself, and doesn't associate with the cubs again, but if the cubs don't have that first experience of denning—if their mother is dead—they don't do it instinctively; they just wander about, forlorn and vulnerable to the elements.)

To return to the killer bears—two such incidents prove nothing conclusive about bear behavior, but there was one interesting similarity in these murders; in neither case did the killer attain its victim by stalking it, or trailing it, or by lying in wait for it; it came on it under fortuitous circumstances, then overwhelmed it by sheer strength and with no necessity for cunning or for any instinctive hunting or killing ability.

The Baker Tract bears don't lend themselves to close or persistent study, so perhaps they do far more killing than I give them blame for, but I don't think so; surely they stumble over new-born fawns every now and then, and devour them on the spot, but if they did much more than that, persistently, I think we would know about it.

Bears have "sign trees." Such a tree—always a softwood conifer in my experience—is to a bear what a "scent post" is to a dog or a fox or a coyote—a specific and established place to deliver the information to others of its species that it has been there, that it was doing business in the general neighborhood, and would probably return. Whereas the canines dispense this information by urinating on the scent post, then kicking up trash around it, bears do it by gnashing the tree with their teeth, as high up as they can reach—anywhere from five to seven feet—so that it is possible for other bears, and incidentally humans, to assess the approximate size and standing height of the particular bear that has left the message. I don't know whether they also urinate around the tree, but I suspect they do—my Labrador used to take a vigorous interest in all bear trees and made an elaborate point of delivering his own message. Nor do I know whether females gnash the trees, but I am quite sure that immature bears do not; on all the trees the marks are so high that only mature animals could have put them there.

All sign trees that I have seen were on well-established and much-used animal runways or on trails made and maintained by humans. (Almost all animals, when passing from one place to another, take the easiest and not necessarily the shortest route, and bears are no different.) The oldest and most-used tree on the tract is a pine standing by a spring on the trail to our Splitrock hunting camp. It is about two feet thick at the butt, and over the years bears have worked on it until now it is chewed more than halfway through.

I like to visit these trees, to know that almost surely there will be tangible evidence that a bear has recently been there. It doesn't help me to divine where it is now or what it might presently be doing; it merely is assurance that it is somewhere about and has no inclination to leave.

Winter

1.

Winter on the tract in Baker's time must have been lonely, drudging hell on the women; for three and sometimes four months, they were locked on the clearing unless they snowshoed eleven miles to the settlement. Except to feed the stock and milk the cows—a chore always relegated to them—they rarely went outside, and Juliet's diary is laced with listless reference to her daily doings: "Mon., Washing, a little of this and that. Tues., the same, read . some. Wed., Commenced me a Napolean [apparently a sort of shawl]. Thurs., doing this and that, wrote a letter. Fri., Read a little, split some wood. Sat., spun some wool. Sun., All day reading."

The men frequently went to town, primarily and ostensibly to pay off taxes by working on the roads, but also, indubitably, to avail themselves of whatever pleasures were available. At such times the women were left behind like a minimal garrison on a frontier outpost; there was one February when Juliet was entirely alone on the clearing while her husband, Wesley Rice, was away: "Tues., Wesley went out. Wed., Wesley not come, blew awful. Thurs., Wesley not home yet. Fri., Wesley still not come. Sat., Wesley come home late. Sun., washed Wesley." After five days of Juliet's frustration, anxiety, and mounting suspicion, I would hate to have been poor Wesley in that wash tub.

Today, winter on the tract is still the time when the men have the best of it, and the women, unless they be exceptional, endure it with patience.

It is also the time, more than any other, when particular weather conditions influence and sometimes dictate what you do.

There is no better way to learn this than on a winter logging operation where inattention to the weather or disregard for what it is likely to be in the near future can make the difference between success and disaster. A thoughtful operator, for instance, will ascertain before snow and frost come precisely where his skid paths and truck roads are going to be; if it is possible to get his tractors in there at the same time (often it is not, due to swampy terrain), he will have roughed out the road, and cleared his loading areas, so that the cutters will arrow the trees diagonally to the paths, and not crosswise or parallel to them; he will cut a substantial amount of the timber he intends to get out as soon as the ground is frozen and before the snow is deep, so that the cutters have optimum working conditions; he will begin to pack down his haul roads with the tractors as soon as heavy frost sets in, but he won't begin to truck logs until the roads are frozen deep and solid; then as soon as the roads are fit, he will truck night and day, around the clock—not trusting the fickle cold weather—to get his logs safely to the mill; and all the while he is doing this, he is quietly and desperately praying that the frost will hold on and that the deep snow will hold off, or at least not come in driblets every day, which would necessitate an interminable plowing and sanding; and all this while he is working against an arbitrary date—March 15—which is the time he can expect a morassing thaw, which might, or might not, be counteracted by another spell of cold weather; in other words, a logger should plan to have his logs, his machinery, and his men out of the woods by that date. There can be no more frantic man than an operator who through lack of planning or the treachery of the weather finds himself caught off base with a thaw in prospect. He is grubbing down through four feet of snow to find the logs hidden beneath, and wallowing them out over unplowed paths to the loading areas that are already plugged with wood; and while he is doing this there are the trucks to be loaded and scaled, and the road to be plowed and sanded; and when there is time to think about it, he is cursing the truck drivers—an independent lot at best—for taking somewhat longer than an eternity to get to the mill and back; and lurking in his mind is the realization that he has lost control of the situation. An operator purely hates a premature spring or even the threat of one.

No two winters are alike; there is the "old-fashioned" type with lasting cold and heavy snow, and there are the mild ones, and all the variations in between. In the winter of 1956, for instance, the deer on the tract never yarded at all—they free-roamed as they do at any other time—and in mid-March, when normally they would have been closeted in the swamps, I found them high on Beaver Mountain, stuffing on beechnuts. The winter of 1961 was unusual and I remember it as I do no other because I was logging a remote area on Kettle Mountain and had my camp at the base of it. This turned out to be a "deep-freeze" spot where the cold settled in and hung on as it did in no other place thereabouts. There was a two-foot snowfall just before Christmas, and then the cold came—unremitting cold—so that the camp thermometer never registered above minus five in the daytime and sank to the low twenties and thirties, and twice went to forty-two, at night. There was no abatement until the fifth of March, but the stranger thing—the almost incredible thing—was that no snow fell after that Christmas storm; the tracks I made just before New Year's, when I was marking the cutting areas, were there and easy to follow, on the first of March. Our only trouble that winter was getting the machinery started in the morning, but we fixed that with a great fire of cull logs, sometimes piled ten feet high, that burned for two months; each night the tractors, trucks, and loader were drawn to its periphery and basked in its warmth and started up in the morning just the way the brochures said they would. That winter was a logger's dream.

As winter is a time for healthy men, so it is also for almost all other vigorous male animals that are carnivorous or omnivorous; starting in early January and continuing through February or later, they are on a compulsive prowl, seemingly aimless, but mostly concerned with procreation. A sparkling subzero day after a fall of dry snow can be a revealing time in the woods; the tracks of dog foxes and coyotes are on every road and clearing and pond shore, leading inevitably to each stub or rock or tuft of grass that makes an obvious scent post; fisher, which are indefatigable night travelers at all times, are abroad in daylight and go on even longer excursions, visiting each and every one of the carrion caches with which they are familiar; male otters are apt to forsake the ponds and streams and go cross-country for miles, short-cutting to possible assignations; buck mink do the same—their loping tracks range far from any water; so also the weasels—one weasel can make enough tracks over a big area to make you believe that a small reconnaissance group of the little monsters are snooping about; and pine marten —just one of them can track up a spruce swamp so that you think a whole company is at large; even a shrew, furrowing just under the snow surface, will crisscross an acre of woods.

By mid-March this frenetic activity is largely over; most of the animals are mated and sated, and spring, although it will be a long time coming, is in view.

2.

As soon as the snow and the cold abate in early spring, there is an apparent proliferation of porcupines on the Baker Tract, especially around the buildings on the clearing, and the various boathouses and camps. This isn't so at all; the animals have been around and about through the winter, and if you had wanted to find them and knew where to look, you could easily have done so, because they don't hibernate—they just sort of stagnate during the bitter weather and exist in morose discomfort.

A few winters ago I was able to keep track of the state of affairs of a certain porcupine residing on the side of Splitrock Ridge; the first time I encountered him was in late November, when I was deer-hunting on snow, and he was ensconced in a great hemlock tree. Subsequently and on four different occasions—the last time was April 4—I passed that way to check on his situation, and each time he was still up there, hadn't come down all winter, and seemed to have no intention of coming down. Why did he stay up there? Was it because the prospects were pleasing, because he was sulking about something, or because he couldn't devise any better way to pass the winter?

Whatever the reason, he was abiding in miserable circumstances—no hole to go into, no shelter from the wind or cold or snow, nothing to eat except what he could get off the hemlock tree. (For those who feel a pang of pity for this beast, I will say that when I went back on May 4 he had abdicated his throne and vanished.)

There was nothing unique about this particular animal; most of the porcupines I've ever seen seemed to take a morbid pleasure in living under the most awful circumstances they could devise for their personal discomfort.

If, for instance, a porcupine takes up residence in a congenial habitat, such as an abandoned woodshed, he won't make the most of his good fortune the way mice do—build a cozy dry nest and all that sort of thing. No, he will proceed instinctively, methodically, and with utter success to foul it up until it is an acrid-stinking place that only he can abide.

The only animals that can live on agreeable terms with porcupines are common rats. They seem to have a mutual regard for each other's vile habits, and when you go into a place, such as an old logging camp, that is accommodating both, it is a loathesome establishment.

Wherever porcupines establish themselves, be it in a rocky ledge with the water seeping in, or in a hollow log, or in a hole under some stump, or under somebody's hunting camp, they have no regard for sanitation, ventilation, or drainage; sooner or later, no matter where, they end up living on a growing mound of their own filth.

Their eating tastes correspond to their living habits. They have a dismal appetite for almost anything that is hard, dry, constipating, and unfit for consumption, unless it be by termites.

And infuriatingly, their most-favored foods are supplied by humans. (But not with that purpose in mind.)

About ten years ago we put up a hunting camp on Splitrock that was sheeted with three-quarter-inch laminated marine plywood. The porcupines ate it—or rather they gnawed it apart to get at the glue—wherever they could get at it, so we put up new plywood and soaked it with creosote. To the porcupines, the creosote seemed to be like catsup on the hamburger, so finally we had to put up metal sheeting.

On a logging job in 1950, the spring thaw came suddenly and much sooner than expected, and stranded one of our tractors in the woods near Beaver Mountain. When we went to retrieve it after mud season, the porcupines had eaten everything they could reach that wasn't metal—the rubber hydraulic tubing, the leather seat cover, and the insulation on the wiring system. (The cost to us of presenting that little smorgasbord was about four hundred dollars.)

On the clearing, porcupines are an infernal and constant nuisance, but most especially in the spring, when they start to wander and seem, inevitably and unerringly, to home on one of the buildings. Once in early April, I watched a huge one come waddling out of the swamp below my house and make a beeline for it, circle it until he found an opening in the foundation, and disappear; he was down there eating weatherboard when I routed him. And another time, again in spring, my Labrador retriever, Adam, was in a mysterious quiet frenzy for two days—he kept lurking under the table in the library and peering into the bookcase that was behind it, and wagging his tail in a tentative sort of way, and occasionally muttering to himself—and I finally got so out of sorts with his nonsense that I moved the table to prove to him that he had better things to do than indulge his imagination. Well, perhaps so, but there was a full-fledged porcupine on the bookshelf, wedged in beside the Encyclopaedia Brittanica, and he (Adam, that is) was delirious at my belated discovery. The porcupine was not; he must have come in through the screen door when Adam and I were asleep, and got confused, and couldn't find his way out, and finally took refuge in the bookcase. Anyway, he was desperate and heaving with fatigue when I finally broomed him out the door.

A porcupine's addiction to the haunts of humans is primarily a yearning for salt in any form—pure salt, brine, sweat (especially from horses), cooking fat impregnated with salt (logging-camp cooks have a tendency to dump their bacon and ham-fat grease in a certain place and this can be attractive to porcupines for years), but I doubt that it is the only thing that attracts them. Why the yen for oil-soaked rubber tubing? For plywood glue? For almost anything that man makes, other than metal, which isn't devised for eating purposes?

Whatever the addiction it is not an easy or pleasant one for we humans on the Baker Tract; no porcupine has ever come that way which improved our environment or peace of mind—except possibly one, and this had to do with an elderly, Victorian, and gargantuan lady who maintained an establishment on the clearing in the early '20s. This was before the days of plumbing, as it is presently defined, and the lady must have resort to the usual privy, molded on the usual modest dimensions, which were not commensurate with her size, stature, or inclinations. Well, a porcupine surveyed her arrangements one night, assessed the plight and inconveniences, and proceeded, on his own volition, to make everything bigger and better—he gnawed away. The old lady, once some sand-papering had been done and her outrage subsided, was delighted—everything was so much easier now—and her son, something of a mother's boy but also with a frolicsome turn of mind, slaughtered the helpful animal, had its head mounted—with all its yellow teeth bared—and gave it to his mother for Christmas. (She treasured it till she died of a spasm.)

Although this predilection to the products of humans is constant and overpowering, it obviously cannot be a necessity or even an important factor in the diet of a porcupine; it has to be in the nature of a windfall. But what they eat in the wilds—what comes naturally—is hardly more succulent.

On the Baker Tract they eat more beech bark than anything else. They also eat tamarack, spruce, pine, and ironwood bark—all of which, interestingly enough, is a last-resort diet for beaver.

Circa 1930—on the left is the great lady for whom a porcupine did a gratuitous but masterful service. The little lady in the center is Squire Baker's daughter, Juliet, aged about ninety-one, with her second husband, William Kellogg, who was somewhat older.

It is almost as if porcupines are predestined to be the pariahs of the woods, forever scourging themselves. But not quite always; sometimes you'll find a porcupine eating something that would be considered excellent fare by some other animals. Sometimes in spring, he'll be in the topmost branches of a poplar or soft maple, swaying in the breeze while he eats the buds. At such times he is apt to express his doleful satisfaction by singing in a soft, rasping monotone that can drive you quietly berserk if you have to listen to it for long. And sometimes you'll find one on the shore of a pond, poking solemn-stupid along a log that juts into the water, stopping occasionally to draw out a lily pad, but these pleasant ventures are only occasional and of short duration.

The mating habits of porcupines are in keeping with their squalid character. On many occasions I have seen pairs of them up in a tree, backing and filling on the branches while they squalled and screeched at each other, and if I hadn't known for sure that they had procreation in mind, I would have thought they were engaged in some sort of sordid slow-motion vendetta; they were going about it with a customary lack of enthusiasm, as if it were just one more cross they had to carry.

In an ecological sense, porcupines seem to have little if any importance on the Baker Tract; they could vanish, or they could proliferate, and it wouldn't make much difference one way or the other. Perhaps it is significant that they never seem to do either; of all the mammals there they are the only one whose numbers seem to remain static, year after year, relatively unaffected by disease, weather, or food circumstances. And they are the only mammal I know that provides nothing essential, and takes nothing essential away. I have read a great deal about how porcupines can devastate a forest by girdling the trees, but it plainly isn't so on the Baker Tract. I've seen thousands of beech and other trees whose stumps have been gnawed by porcupines, but I've seen only four or five where the trees have been girdled the whole way round, which is essential if the trees are to be killed. I've seen instances where a porcupine has climbed a tamarack or a spruce or a white pine and killed it by almost denuding it of bark, but this doesn't happen often and the consequences to the forest are paltry.

A porcupine is not dependent on any other living animal, and I doubt that any animal is dependent on or influenced by the relative prevalence of porcupines, in other words there is no such a thing as a coyote-rabbit or fox-mouse relationship wherein the abundance of one can affect the abundance or scarcity of the other.

The only animal on the tract that preys with any regularity on porcupines is the fisher. In winter, if you follow a fisher track far enough, it will take you to a dead porcupine. You'll find it, or rather its pelt, quill-side down, laid out on the ground as neatly as a bath mat. A fisher will come back to such a kill time after time, long after the meat and bones have been consumed. But there is for me an inexplicable thing about this—in the last ten years fisher have made an incredible comeback on the Baker Tract, (up to 1940 I saw only one, in the last few years I've seen about twenty-five)—but the increase in numbers doesn't seem to have influenced the porcupine population at all.

I know that bobcats kill an occasional porcupine—a friend of mine saw one do it. He was fishing on the river when he noticed it out again, as though it were gently stroking something, then a bobcat on the far shore; it was standing in front of a rock crevice, much absorbed, and poking one paw inside, and drawing suddenly it leaped and drew out an almost dead porcupine by the head. Whether the bobcat achieved this by "stroking" it or by biting it my friend never knew—he couldn't ford the river to find out.

I think coyotes and red foxes may occasionally kill a porcupine, but I don't know this; I've trapped several of each with quills in them, but that isn't substantial proof, because they may merely have been feeding on the carcass. I assume, but again I don't know, that bears, if sufficiently aroused and hungry, will have a go at one. Under aggravating circumstances a bear will tackle almost anything—bees, hornets, boar pigs—why not porcupines?

But the fact remains that on the Baker Tract porcupines don't seem to have cycles of scarcity or abundance; year after year they are in the expected places and in the usual numbers. They seem unmindful of, and impervious to, outside influences; they just go their own way—moody, despicable, unloved, and not necessary.

Despite their stolid boorishness, they have a curiosity of a sort. There is no better way to discover this than by operating a fox or coyote trap line. Lures for these animals are of the stinky sexy glandular type, not pure meat baits such as you'd use for fisher or bobcats or coons, and porcupines are forever bumbling around them and getting into the traps. The first time I ran into this situation I took laborious pains to release the wretched thing, but the next night I caught it again in a similar set about twenty-five feet away. (Porcupines are not the only herbivorous animal that has a fascination for these sets—cattle, especially steers, are drawn to them, and so also are such animals as woodchucks and red squirrels and deer.)

Porcupines are as insensible to physical discomfort, apparently, as anything can be, and if you want proof of this, try smoking one out of a hollow tree. I attempted it once; Adam, the Labrador, came home in agony one winter afternoon with his face and neck and throat a ghastly pincushion of quills, and after we'd done the best we could for him (it took four of us to hold him down while another man yanked out the quills with tweezers), I backtracked my dog to a hollow beech tree where the porcupine was holed up. Now then, smoking anything out of a home place is a mean, dirty business, but I tried it anyway; I kindled an impressive smudge that soon sent columns of smoke seeping from every knothole and crack, then I sat back to await developments, and the porcupine. Neither was forthcoming; I couldn't even hear it scratching around in there. I continued this foul treatment until dark—about two hours—then I put out the fruitless smudge and went home. When I returned a month later, the porcupine was still in residence and seemed to be taking the usual moody displeasure in his good health.

I doubt that anyone can learn to love a porcupine; you can feel sorry for them, or be disgusted, and occasionally loathe them, and sometimes you can even laugh at one; a porcupine on a ponderous progress through the woods, like some old imperial wizard marching to a secret meeting of the clan—eyes front, spraddle-legged, flat-footed, with its tail going from side to side like shifting ballast, and its murky emotions fixed on hallucinations of earth-stirring proportions—is a comical sight.

But at best you think of them as being long-suffering and of little goodness.

3.

One sunny bitter-cold afternoon in February, I saw a strange animal from my office window; it was far off and floundering through the snow toward the alder swamp beyond my lawn. It seemed to be about the size and shape of a small hound.

For a few seconds I was confused as to what it was; the idea that it might be a fox or a small coyote or a bobcat crossed my mind, but it was obviously none of these things, so I went for the field glasses.

It was, in fact, a beagle hound—a possibility that hadn't entered my head because the clearing is a small island of human occupancy surrounded and isolated by a sea of wilderness, so it is rare indeed that a domesticated animal of any sort finds its way there.

As it angled closer, I saw that it had a collar and a dog tag, and that it was a male. When I went out on the porch and called to it, he stopped instantly and looked in my direction, then when I called again, he made a frenzied dash for the swamp and disappeared.

Sighting this dog cleared up a mystery—ever since New Year's we had been seeing its tracks about the clearing, and several times it had come to my meat caches, but no one had seen it, so, lacking a better explanation, we assumed that a coyote had taken up residence in the vicinity. (It would be unusual for a coyote to do this, because they aren't apt to be loners and aren't addicted to human habitations.) But this beagle, as it turned out, behaved in an even more bizarre way.

I backtracked it and discovered that it had spent the night—or perhaps longer than that—underneath one of the summer cottages. I left part of a beaver carcass, presuming it would be back, and went home.

The beaver meat wasn't touched and the hound never returned to that particular cottage, but a week later I came across his tracks and again followed them back; he had come from beneath another cottage and had apparently spent considerable time there. I left another chunk of meat, but he didn't return for it, nor did he come to my meat caches again.

Three mornings later after a fresh snow, I found his tracks again; they came from the swamp, went across the clearing, and under the crawl space of still a third cottage. When I circled the place and knew for a certainty that he was still under there, I went home for a flashlight and some more meat, but when I came back there were fresh tracks coming from the crawl space—lunging, up-to-the-belly troughs in the snow which showed he had left that place in a desperate hurry.

We never saw him again, or any sign of him—he simply fled to the woods and vanished without trace. Since then I've wondered about him—where he came from, how he got to the clearing, and why he came to behave in that feral way.

I suppose he was someone's rabbit hound and that he got lost while hunting, and eventually found his way to the clearing. I think this despite my knowing most of the rabbit hunters in the vicinity, none of whom reported him missing or even knew of such a lost dog, and despite the fact he seemed to take no interest in rabbits—we would surely have heard him yapping if he had been active in this respect—and despite the fact that during the seven weeks that we were aware of his presence on the clearing, he seemed actually to shun our open road, preferring to make his own way through the heavy snow. (This is particularly queer because even the wariest animals—bears, deer, bobcats, coyotes, and foxes—have no aversion to our thoroughfares and use them for their convenience, especially in winter.)

Some people have advanced the theory that this beagle had been mistreated and, as a consequence, had run away from home. I doubt it, for plenty of neglected or mistreated dogs drift away from home and become semiwild, or even truly feral, but in my experience they always do it in conjunction with another dog or a pack—never alone. All dogs I've known lose their initiative and enthusiasm when left to their own solitary resources.

No matter how or why or from whence this beagle came to the clearing, it was remarkable, but his way of life after that was inexplicable. Had he become truly feral, or was he merely existing in a bewildered and terrified state? Why did he creep under those cottages—always deserted, never the same one— but shun all human association? Why was he as leary of my meat offerings as a smart coyote would be of a clumsily baited trap? I don't know; all I know is that he was an animal in limbo —lost somewhere between the human world and the wilderness, and unable to adjust to either.

To my knowledge, the only other domesticated animals that have found their way to the clearing were another dog and two cats. The dog was a huge curly-haired black animal who arrived unannounced and from only he knew where, and instantly and for all time attached himself to John Byrne, who was then boss. They were inseparable—except twice daily when Buster went to fetch the cows—and he was the most affectionate, considerate, and satisfactory dog that ever I knew on the clearing.

The cats, one a black female and the other a ginger-colored tom, were strays from abandoned logging camps. The black one came five miles across woods and swamps and around ponds, without benefit of any road or trail, from Blackwell's Stillwater, and for twelve years she led a curious life on or about the clearing. During the warm-weather times she led a feral existence and was rarely seen, but the first bitter weather would bring her to the farmhouse door, meowing for admittance, and there she would remain, dignified and patient and smug as only a cat can be, lapping milk, drowsing, catching a mouse when she felt like it—but not really working at it—and then when warm weather came and she had no further use for this association, she simply departed to take up another life in the vicinity of the clearing. I used to see her in the pasture from time to time, prowling for game or squatting on a rock, and when she knew she was under surveillance she was as chary and furtive as a fox. One autumn, she failed to show up at the farmhouse.

A few years later, in January, the ginger tom found his way to the clearing; he had come cross-country from our logging camp beyond Thumb Pond. We had shut down the camp in September, so it had taken him about four months to find his way. Unlike the black female, which condescended to human association when convenient, this tom would have none of it— he was more like the beagle—he lurked about and was forever furtive. The only way we knew of his presence—except for rare sightings—was from his tracks in the snow, going under an unoccupied cottage, visiting the horse barn, investigating the garbage dump, but always privately and usually at night, like a foreign agent engaged in covert affairs.

The domesticated animals and fowl that were brought to the clearing, as opposed to the two cats and two dogs that arrived of their own volition, either succumbed quickly or were dispensed with as being unsuitable or unnecessary, or else they prospered and were useful.

Turkeys, due to their stupidity, tempting size, and unawareness, fared the worst. Juliet Baker's diary was, for the first few months, laced with doleful references to them: "Hen turkey is setting." . . . "Something et up my turkey eggs. . . . Hen turkey setting again. . . . Hen turkey hatched eight eggs, something et up five. . . . Wolves come, et up my hen turkey and the chicks. . . . Company come to dinner. I baked the gobbler." The last effort to raise them ended when they perished en masse in a sleet storm, apparently preferring that fate to going into their adjacent shed.

The Bakers brought sheep with them and for the first few years the wolves plagued them unmercifully, but when the wolves disappeared from the tract, the sheep thrived, and their wool and meat were almost invaluable. After the Bakers' departure, sheep continued on the clearing for many years, but we dispensed with them during the war, fortunately I think, because it is doubtful they could have survived the influx of coyotes or the increase in bears.

Sometime in the early 1900s two Mexican burros were brought to the clearing by an elderly gentleman, of huge size but short of stamina, to transport him and his baggage to and from his fishing camp on the river. The burros survived these onerous burdens, but the cold of the following winter was too much for them and they perished.

Twenty years later, a donkey named Eleanor arrived under the auspices of another elderly gentleman who was cantankerous, opinionated, and as much an ass as Eleanor. His idea about Eleanor was that she would take the back work and drudgery out of hunting by carrying the provisions and lugging home the dead deer. Well, it turned out that Eleanor had an irreconcilable aversion to dead deer—she would kick and bite wildly when in the vicinity of one, and, despite everything that's been said about the surefootedness of the species, she was as clumsy in the woods as a duck on glare ice, at least when there was a pack on her back. On one occasion at Splitrock Pond, Eleanor, briefly untended, went tripping out on a log that extended into deep water, and suddenly capsized upside down—it took all available hands to get her right side up and back to shore with the lunch.

Despite this sort of behavior and despite the fact that she was addicted to braying—a grievous, discordant, soul-shivering crescendo of anguish that could be heard about the clearing and from miles away—Eleanor remained for two years, at the old man's petulant insistence, then even he got the message and donated her to a Boy Scout camp, located seventy miles to the south, out of sight and mind and hearing.

So it was the basic frontier livestock—sheep, pigs, chickens, cows, and horses—that not only survived and prospered but were eminently useful to the Bakers.

Pigs seem to have been the easiest to maintain. Juliet, who detailed every misfortune that befell the clearing animals, had only this to relate about pigs—"All day butchering and salting the hogs."

They too were kept on the clearing after the Bakers departed, and there was nothing remarkable or memorable about any of them except for three shoats, named Ethyl, Myrtle, and Mac, which John Byrne raised one summer. For some whimsical reason he didn't confine them to the pigpen, so in short order they were following him about in company with his two dogs— going on the garbage detail, hiking to Splitrock when he went there to paint a canoe, following the wagon to the sawmill when he went there for lumber—and when he wasn't about, they foraged far and wide through the woods. There was a fine crop of beechnuts that fall and Ethyl, Myrtle, and Mac gorged on them so that they were proclaimed the finest pork ever raised on Baker's Clearing.

The Bakers' chickens were free-roaming. They must have been targets for every fox, owl, hawk, weasel, and coon, but Juliet had surprisingly little to say about it—she was much more irked by the hens, which secretly went off to the woods and "stole" their nests.

In more recent years, the chickens have been confined and are like chickens everywhere—myopic, self-centered, prone to hysteria, and most satisfactory.

The clearing cattle never had any aversion to or fear of the wilderness. "Four days looking for Beulah," wrote Juliet. "Found her down to Mink swamp with bull calf. Carried him back," and ever since then expecting mothers have continued this infuriating habit. Steers, heifers, and bulls, unless accompanied by milking cows, will take to the woods and wander for miles and often have no inclination at all to come back. They seem to have no sense of home, the way horses do, and are indifferent to human association unless they are being fed, or need to be milked, or want shelter from the elements.

It is conceivable that the Bakers could have made some sort of life on the clearing without pigs, chickens, cows, and sheep; it would have been impossible without horses for transport, land-clearing, plowing, and hauling logs. The Bakers' horses were their most prized possessions.

They arrived on the clearing with two bred mares. (Baker paid $350 for them, which is precisely what we paid for a good team ninety years later), and horses, or at least one horse, have been on the clearing ever since. Their usefulness, due to machinery, has declined almost to the point where it is a luxury to keep them, but there are still things to do in the woods and about the clearing that a horse can manage far better than a tractor.

For a horse to be of any use in the woods, he has to be solid, honest, and sensible; a skittish silly horse that panics when a partridge flushes, or has a mortal fear of deer, or imagines every rotting stump to be a bear, or gets lonely and desperate when left to itself—such a horse is worthless and dangerous.

Ten years ago, and briefly, we had such a horse; he not only had all of these faults, but he also lacked any sense of direction, so that he was constantly getting himself lost in the woods. When this happened, he would set up a baleful whinnying which he kept up until someone came to steer him home. He wandered off one day during deer season and was incommunicado for a week until two hunters, returning to their camp on Nate Pond from a day's sport, discovered the brute in residence—he had broken into their stores and devoured what the poor devils had hoped was a two-week bread supply. The horse was overjoyed to see them and almost trampled them to death in his manifestations of affection and gratitude.

Except for this abysmal animal, the clearing horses, once they feel at home, never go far into the woods or stay away for long, whether or not they are being fed, and sometimes, but rarely, there is a "one-man horse" that is totally reliant on its owner and is destitute without him. About ten years ago, we hired a man named Whitey LeJoie to cut pulp, and he brought his own horse in preference to using one of ours. Also, instead of using our accommodations, he constructed his own—a shack made of spruce poles and paper cartons—far out in the woods and close to his cutting area—and that is where he and the horse, Tom, lived for two years.

I never knew two more adept workers; when they skidded pulp poles together, it was a graceful symphonic thing—no shouting, no backing and filling, just a quiet rapport on what the business was about.

Whitey was a sporadic drunk and every two weeks he went to town for three days or more, during which time Tom haunted his shack and foraged close by rather than come to the clearing to graze.

One Saturday noon during that second October, Whitey came to see me. He said he was through with woods life forever and wouldn't be back. We could have Tom, he said.

I thought he was merely disgruntled and that a few days in town would make him feel better, so, joking, I asked where he was going.

"The Bowery," he said. "I been there once. I think I go back."

We never saw or heard of him again. For a month or so, we expected him to show up, and Tom did too; one of us went out to the camp daily to bring him in for a feed of oats, but he always went back to stand, morose and patient, by the shack. It wasn't until snow came that we finally put him in the barn, and after that and for five years, he was the best horse we had.

Of all domesticated animals that have been regularly on the clearing, dogs have caused the most problems. This is not because the place isn't a dog's idea of heaven on earth, but precisely for that reason; if allowed to go their own irresponsible and turbulent ways, then soon become obnoxious and sometimes impossible. This is because any dog, regardless of its size, can put mortal fear into almost any animal, including bears and most especially deer, and almost all dogs have a natural inclination to kill (or perhaps it's unnatural) for the mere enjoyment of it.

The Bakers brought no dogs with them, probably because they would serve no useful purpose and there was nothing for them to eat which the Bakers themselves could not utilize. Later, when the Bakers were established, deerhounds were brought in, but apparently this was more for the enjoyment of the city "sports"—some of whom delighted in being paddled close up to a driven deer, then blowing its brains out—than for any practical advantage to the Bakers; they had other and better ways to get venison, so dogs were always on a peripheral status; they were comforting companions when they behaved but dispensable if they didn't.

It is the same today except that the prevalence of deer makes the situation far more difficult. In Baker's time they were scarce, and anyone that ventured on the clearing did so in mortal peril, but today they are forever about in greater or lesser numbers—one clear February afternoon I counted sixty-seven that had come from the swamp to bask in the sun—and they are

Only a thoroughly disciplined dog can resist these temptations!

an irresistible temptation to any dog that hasn't been forcibly trained to leave them alone.

Most puppies are easily trained; Charlie, the boss, presently has a Boston terrier who is most compatible with the semitame deer that are constantly about the farmhouse. There is an old doe named Pauline who gives him a washing with her tongue whenever they encounter each other, and then he reciprocates the favor, standing with his forepaws on her side and reaching as high as he can. Sometimes he chases the other deer, then they chase him.

Older dogs are harder to train. I had a bad time with my Labrador, Adam—he was a lusty, hardheaded animal and I beat him many times, unmercifully but to no avail, whenever he chased a deer. I finally tied a fresh deer hide to his collar and let him drag it about for two days. This treatment made him psychopathic about deer for a short time; if he saw one coming, he'd skulk away, hangdog, to where he couldn't see it or have it on his mind, but he got over this trauma and thereafter manifested a massive disdain for all deer, confining his interests to the frenzied fruitless pursuit of red squirrels, the farm cats, and an occasional porcupine.

The influence of the clearing on Adam was interesting in two other respects—before he came there he had been a great roamer and sometimes would travel cross-country for miles and be gone for days, but after he came to the clearing, he was never tempted to leave it on his own hook; apparently the place was so remote that no tantalizing smells of other dogs were ever wafted to him. On the other hand this very remoteness from other dogs, at least male dogs, finally made him insanely jealous of them; after a year or so of being boss dog on the clearing, he would attack, with intent to kill, any male that came for a visit. I finally had to destroy him.

The dogs that are almost impossible to deer-break are those that have been allowed to run them with impunity; once a dog has killed one and tasted the blood, there isn't anything to be done except confine him or get rid of him.

There were two such dogs on the clearing, briefly, in 1947. They came from the farm country far to the south of us and were reputed by their owner to be great ratters and wood-chuckers. Well, there were none of either species on the clearing, so the dogs became interested in deer.

Those two animals were improbable villains; one was an oafish Thurber-type spaniel who drooled constantly and went galumphing about like an iron horse; the other was a feisty mutt that weighed no more than seventeen pounds, dripping wet.

They were amusing and fun to have around, and when they absented themselves from time to time it was assumed that they were engaged in innocuous business having to do with chipmunks and red squirrels and such, but they weren't—they were clandestine pursuers (both were silent trailers) and killers of deer. We were cutting ice on Mink Pond one February day when they chased a large buck out of the woods and brought it to bay in the middle of the pond. Before we could get there, they had hamstrung it and brought it down, and we had, literally, to beat them senseless to get them away from it, too late of course. They were forthwith deported to their place of origin.

Until a few years ago, the heterogeneous assortment of clearing livestock had never included tame rabbits or hares. This situation changed abruptly and without prior notice; a far neighbor brought in some heifers to summer on our pasture, and while the maidens were being off-loaded, a great hare, black as a devil, tumbled from the truck and scurried off. Our friend explained that this creature had been an Easter present for his children but had alienated their affection because it was a biter. He proclaimed it to be a buck rabbit.

Two days later, another neighbor drove up with more heifers and some steers and a bull—and a pure white rabbit. (We don't know to this day whether this intrusion of rabbits was a weird circumstance or a collusive mischief on the part of the two men.) At any rate, the white rabbit instantly sought the company of the black one, and thereafter were known as May Britt and Sammy Davis, respectively, and were inseparable.

Their arrival was met with dour prognostications a) as to their fate, and b) as to the future of Baker's Clearing if they survived. It was assumed by almost everybody that they were living on borrowed time. Some people gave them until no later than tomorrow morning by sunup; others surmised that it might take a week for an owl or a goshawk or a coyote or a fox or a bobcat to do them in; a few blithe optimists thought they might survive a month.

Only one lady, horrified by their presence, took the view that they would persist like evil genies and populate, not only the clearing, but the whole Adirondacks, with pinto rabbits, and spotted ones, and probably dirty gray ones as well. "They'll be worse than rats because they're much bigger," she said. She remained convinced of this even when it became evident that May Britt was a female impersonator.

Sammy and May were untroubled by these ominous predictions and went their charmed innocent way, always together, like virgins in a Mafia bordello. They allowed no one to touch them, they were standoffish about profferings of food such as carrots and lettuce, and they never established a permanent home place. One day they would be living under the horse barn, a week later they might be in residence under my brother's house, a quarter of a mile away, then they would transfer to some other accommodation. There was no telling where they would be, or why—they were forever making unexpected visitations, then departing elsewhere without notice or apparent purpose.

Albeit they were not of athletic conformation, they were dedicated travelers. The clearing is about a mile long and a quarter mile wide, and they traversed it all, and frequently took to the woods surrounding it. One day I was coming up the trail from Mink Pond when I encountered the two coming down it, clumping along with solemn-stupid intent. They passed by without so much as nodding so I have no idea what they had in mind, but they were back on the clearing the next morning.

All that first summer, Sammy and May cruised about the clearing like idiot tourists with no apparent interest in people, other animals, or elegant cuisine. Almost everybody, at one time or another, tried to captivate them with delicious offerings, but to no avail—they seemed to prefer whatever haphazard coarse fare they chanced upon. Despite this rude behavior, the clearing people took a jealous interest in their welfare—as if they were distinguished, albeit incomprehensible, visitors from outer space. Charlie Kays, the boss, proclaimed that the environment around his establishment was their preferred hostelry and that they always returned to it, sooner or later, after their frivolous sorties. When they took up quarters under my brother's house, my brother was quite smug about it and let it be known that he had a certain congenial atmosphere that no others of us could provide, and when they departed after two weeks, leaving him flat, and transferred to the crawl space under my outbuilding, he couldn't conceal his hurt and disgust. It went on that way all summer, and the lady referred to above was the only person who wished them ill, turned away at their appearance, and incanted against them.

It was generally assumed that winter would see the end of them—snow, cold, lack of food, predators—however could they survive? Obviously they couldn't, but they did, and without assistance from anybody. For five bleak snowbound months they existed, or perhaps prospered, and when spring came, there they were. There was one important difference, however—they were out of sorts with each other and leading separate lives—they were like two stranded mariners on a small island who refuse to pool their resources or even recognize that the other exists. They didn't hate each other, they merely ignored one another, and were self-sufficient and apparently myopically content.

They had become more sedentary. May took up semipermanent residence under my outbuilding, and Sammy established himself under Charlie's horse barn, and only occasionally did they go on tours, but one afternoon I watched them pass each other on the road by the icehouse—they seemed oblivious of each other.

One September evening, two friends and I were sitting at my kitchen window and were parties to a strange incident. We were watching two deer licking intently on the salt stumps when May appeared from under the outbuilding and positioned himself about ten feet from the deer, seeming to study them, then suddenly he darted forward and launched a series of capers—around their noses, under their bellies and behind their tails. At first the deer made a show of indifference to these antics (deer have about as much humor as Aunt Jemima Puddleduck), but then, inexplicably, they started to play with that incongruous rabbit; they made mock strikes at him with their front feet, and put their heads down as if to butt him, then they played a sort of tag game, chasing May one minute, allowing themselves to be chased the next.

When it was all over, the deer went back to the salt, and May resumed his stolid existence, but just for a few moments there, a spark of desperation—a yearning, for recognition and status—seemed to have ignited that forlorn rabbit.

When the snow went off after their second winter, Charlie found Sammy's body, intact, near the horse barn. Maybe a weasel had killed him and merely sucked the blood, or perhaps he starved, or died of the cold, or old age.

May lived through the third summer and well into the following winter under my outbuilding. I had learned by that time that his real food passion was for suckers and prunings from my wild apple trees, and once he found them and came to count on them, he never left the premises for long. (In the beginning I had cut and piled these branches to beguile the deer and the family of snowshoe hares that live under my house, but May was never about when the deer or the hares were feeding on them—he had apparently become a psychopathic loner.)

When I left in March, May was still living under the outbuilding, but he wasn't there when I came back in late April, and we never found any trace of him.

I doubt that the saga of Sammy and May proves much of anything, and I am not about to write some symbolic or fabulous meaning into it—they were merely useless animals that had been dumped, literally, on the clearing with no purpose, good or bad, projected for them, and with no conceivable capacity in them to do either. They were clowns, which is to say that they were adaptable, and, unlike other animals that came to Baker's Clearing, they were never taken for granted.